Stop Foreclosure

Stop Foreclosure

How to Get a Loan Modification

Introduction 6

Should I Apply for a Modification Before I am No Longer Able to Make My Mortgage Payment? 10

What Do I Need to Show to Get a Modification to My Loan? 13

What are the Two Most Important Considerations for Whether I Will Succeed in Getting My Mortgage Modified to a Lower Payment? 15

I am Currently Unemployed and Have No Prospects of a Job. What are My Chances of Getting My Home Loan Modified? 27

What Hit on My Credit Rating Will I Take For Not Making My Mortgage Payments? 28

What Documentation Will I Be Required to Produce? 28

How Much Income Must I Show to Qualify for a Modification? 38

Can I Protect my Savings, IRAS and Health Savings Accounts? 40

What are My Chances for Getting My Mortgage Loan Modified If I Currently Have No Income as I Just Lost My Job, but am Certain I Will Land Gainful Employment Soon? 41

©Robert Rodgers, PhD

Stop Foreclosure

I Just Landed A Good Job. Why was My Application for a Modification to My Mortgage Denied? 43

What Mortgage Payment Can I Qualify For? 45

Guidelines for Reporting Expenses 48

What are the Most Common Reasons for Requesting a Modification? 50

Who Are the Players When It Comes to Getting My Mortgage Modified? 52

How Can I Determine Who Services My Home Mortgage and Who Owns My Mortgage Note? 57

My Mortgage Servicer Tells Me that the Owner of My Note is Different from What I see on my Original Mortgage Note. Can This Be True? 58

Can I Determine who Owns My Mortgage Note By Searching Deeds of Trust Filed with My County Courthouse? 59

What is MERS? 59

I Do Not Suspect that My Mortgage Servicing Company Has the Original Loan Documents. Why Can't I just Demand that They Produce the Original Documents? When They Can't Produce the Original Documents (as I Suspect) Doesn't My Loan Also Vanish and I Get My Home for Free? 61

Should I Hire Someone Else to Handle My Application for a Mortgage Loan Application? 64

How Can I Avoid Being Scammed? 67

©Robert Rodgers, PhD

Stop Foreclosure

Why Did We Get a Foreclosure Notice when Our Mortgage Servicer was Still Evaluating Our Application for a Modification?...67

Why Do I have So Much Difficulty Dealing with My Mortgage Servicer? 69

What Happens When I Contact My Mortgage Servicer About Applying for a Modification? 70

What Can I Expect when Calling My Mortgage Servicer? 71

Why Can't I Email the Documents to My Mortgage Servicer? It Would Be So Much Easier...77

What Can I Do to Hurry Up the Review Process and Get a Decision More Quickly? We have been Hassling with Our Mortgage Servicer Now for Over a Year 79

How Exactly Can My Mortgage Be Modified to Reduce My Monthly Payments?..84

Am I Eligible to Apply for a Federal Making Home Affordable Modification?..88

Will I Qualify for a Modification to My Home Loan that is Underwritten by the Federal HAMP Program?.....................90

Is Equity Advantageous or Disadvantageous When It Comes to Getting My Home Loan Modified? 98

What is the Principal Behind a Net Present Value Analysis? 100

How Do I Determine the Current Market Value of My Home? 102

©Robert Rodgers, PhD

Stop Foreclosure

How Do I Dispute a Market Analysis of My Home that Has Disqualified Me from Getting a Modification 105

What is a Discount Rate? 109

How Can I Calculate the Net Present Value (NPV) 111

How Can I Find Out My Credit Score for Free? 115

After Entering All My Information into a Net Present Value Analysis - I Failed. What Can I Do Now? 117

Will it Really Help Me Obtain a Modification to My Home Mortgage If Go to All the Trouble of Doing My Own Net Present Value Analysis? 118

I Know Precisely the Mortgage Payment I Can Handle for the Next Several Years. Once I Dig Myself Out of the Mess I am In Right Now, I will be Able to Pay the Original Amount. Should I Ask My Mortgage Servicer to Consider a Two Year (or Short Term) Modification? I Know Now I Will Only Need to Pay the Reduced Amount for a Couple of Years. 121

How Will I Hear About the Outcome of My Application? 123

Will My Mortgage Servicer Give me a Reason for a Denial? 128

How Can I Dispute Penalties or Late Fees Charged by My Mortgage Servicer? 129

My Mortgage Servicer Says that Extending the Term of My Loan from 30 to 40 Years is Not an Option. Are They Bluffing? 130

What Are My Options If My Income Does Not Justify a Modified Loan? 132

©Robert Rodgers, PhD

Stop Foreclosure

I am Currently Unemployed. Is There any Hope for Me? What Programs Exist for People Who Want to Remain in Their Homes? 133

How Do I Find Out If Freddie Mac Owns My Loan? 136

I was offered a Temporary Modification but was only One (1) Day Late Making the Second Payment. We were Serviced a Foreclosure Notice Today. Can the Bank Foreclosure Now When They have Already Agreed to a Modification? 136

The Bank Has Offered a Modification but the Rate is Still Too Much for My Pocketbook. They Say that They Cannot Offer me a HAMP (the federal program which would make the payment more affordable) because I Have Been Delinquent in Making Payments for More than One Year. Should I just Give Up Now? 137

What is a Three Month Temporary Loan Modification? I Asked for a Permanent Modification to my Mortgage Loan. 138

Is the Deal Done When I Get a Written Offer of a Modification? 139

I was told by a Clerk about the Terms of a Temporary Modification but Cannot Tell if this is a Genuine Offer. The Offer Seemed Very Unprofessional to Me. 141

What Can I Realistically Expect If a Modification is Offered? How Much Lower Can I Expect My Payment to Be? 141

Aren't the Mortgage Companies the Bad Guys Here? 144

©Robert Rodgers, PhD

Stop Foreclosure

What if I also have a Second Mortgage or Line of Credit on the Property? 145

How Do I Find a Housing Counselor? 146

Are the Laws Governing Modifications to Mortgages Really That Complicated? 148

My Mortgage Servicing Company Refuses to Offer a Modification to My Loan that I am Fully Qualified to Receive (by My Own Calculation) Under the Net Present Value Test. What Can I Do? 149

Foreclosure Process 150

Judicial Versus Non-Judicial Foreclosures 152

Foreclosures 153

FHA Loan Modifications 155

Other Options to Avoid Foreclosure 157

Foreclosure 165

Bankruptcy 167

Mediation 168

Useful Resources 171

Index 172

©Robert Rodgers, PhD

Stop Foreclosure

Introduction

I recently analyzed the books that are available to people seeking a modification to their home mortgage. Unemployment strikes out of the blue at times, as do health challenges, making the obligation to pay a mortgage payment impossible. The shock to me was that none of the books tell you what you need to know and do to be successful.

Some of the books tell you how to complete the forms. Others copy the federal regulations on loan modifications which are free anyway. Still other companies offer to hold your hand through the process for an outrageous fee. From my experience, none of this information or help for that matter really helps a hill of beans. How do I know this?

What is my experience in these matters? First, I actually experienced the process of securing a loan modification for my own home. The process took a year and a half. I was successful in the end, but the journey to success was fraught with frustration and angst. I wish I had known then what I know today when I initiated the process.

©Robert Rodgers, PhD

Stop Foreclosure

Second, I have since been certified as a senior foreclosure mediator for the state of Washington. Having now mediated quite a few foreclosure cases, I have a firm handle on what you are up against, the odds that you will be successful. More importantly I have a good sense of what mortgage servicing companies are willing to do for you.

I realized one day that I have a vast experience and knowledge about this process of getting a mortgage modified that I need to share with others. What you hear from mortgage servicers or read about on websites is now how the process actually works.

How to Get a Home Loan Modification in These Crazy Times was written as a guide to home owners interested in succeeding with an application for modification to their mortgage which reduces the payments that they owe each and every month. This book explains everything you need to know to succeed and if success if not likely, your options are covered.

Two years ago I succeeded in obtaining a permanent modification to our home mortgage.

©Robert Rodgers, PhD

Stop Foreclosure

Our modification reduced the loan interest on our mortgage three percentage points from 6.75%, the percent set on our original loan, to 3.375%. This reduction made the monthly payments affordable.

I learned important lessons about how to get a loan modification during the year and a half negotiation process which I now share with you. I only wish I had known what I know now before I even initiated the loan modification process. To be perfectly clear, I really did not approach the application process intelligently. I made many mistakes along the way which helped me identify the correct way to proceed. You now get to benefit from my mistakes. The length of the application process could have been cut in half.

My intention with this book is to provide you with all the information you need to succeed. It is not an easy process, nor is it pleasant. But the effort can be well worth the outcome.

Be forewarned that even under the best of circumstances getting a loan modification approved is not a simple or speedy process. It takes time, perseverance and patience. You will

©Robert Rodgers, PhD

Stop Foreclosure

be lucky if you get an answer within a year after you initiate the application.

It is important to understand what you are up against, including a simple explanation of the different business interests that are involved in the process. My book offers a unique set of recommendations that will increase your chances of success if you decide to proceed with a modification request with your loan servicer. I am teaching you all the lessons I learned the hard way. I really had no idea what I was getting myself into you. In this book, I explain exactly what you are up against and why.

Robert Rodgers, Ph.D.
Olympia, Washington

Should I Apply for a Modification Before I am No Longer Able to Make My Mortgage Payment?

I initially called the company that serviced my mortgage (GMAC) before I had even missed a mortgage payment. It had become clear that a temporary illness in the family would hamper my

Stop Foreclosure

ability to make the monthly mortgage payments. I had this silly idea that GMAC would honor my integrity and openness. Because I had always paid on time in the past, they would be willing to work with me to secure a temporary modification which needed to extend only a couple of years. I knew it would not take me long to get back on track.

I had learned from my internet research that to qualify for a federal HAMP program, I must have never been late paying my monthly mortgage obligation. I thus decided that the only rational strategy was to apply for a modification before I had ever missed making a payment. In addition, I was also interested in obtaining favorable terms over the short term – which is precisely what a HAMP modification does. Your interest rate actually creeps up over five years before settling on a much higher rate at the end of the five year period when the relief period is exhausted.

I called my mortgage service company (GMAC) and explained that my family was confronting some temporary health challenges which had reduced our ability to generate enough income to

Stop Foreclosure

meet our monthly mortgage commitment. I requested consideration for a temporary HAMP modification. I explained that after two years, I was confident I would be able to pay the original commitment in a timely and reliable fashion. I also explained to the phone representative that my understanding about HAMP was that I could not be late making a payment to apply.

The problem with my strategy was that I had never been late with my payments. The GMAC service representative explained that the only chance I might have with getting a modification was to stop making my mortgage payments. As long as I was paying my mortgage on time, I did not have a prayer of succeeding with a modification. He explained that if a home owner can still pay their monthly mortgage, they need not even bother initiating a request for a modification.

I explained that I would prefer not to take a hit on my credit rating. He said that I had no choice. My only chance to obtain a modification of a loan at a lower rate was to stop making payments, apply

©Robert Rodgers, PhD

Stop Foreclosure

for a modification and accept a big hit in our credit rating.

I took his advice. I stopped making my monthly payment and applied for a modification. This was only the beginning of the process. The modification was ultimately approved, but the process from beginning to end took a year and a half later.

The bottom line is that to be considered seriously, you will have to stop making your payments. And, if you have any savings or cash reserves, your servicer will claim you do have the ability to pay your mortgage. You can claim that the cash reserves are needed to pay for the health treatments but that argument will fall on deaf ears. You will be taken seriously if you stop paying your mortgage and have no fallback in the form of savings or other cash reserves.

What Do I Need to Show to Get a Modification to My Loan?

A mortgage loan modification is a written agreement between the home owner and the lender that permanently changes one or more of

Stop Foreclosure

the original terms of the mortgage note. They are considered when the home owner:

1. Has a stable source of income to support a modified level of monthly payment monthly.
2. Desires to retain ownership of the home
3. Has encountered an inability to pay the current mortgage due to involuntary circumstances such as temporary unemployment, health issues, divorce or other unanticipated financial obligations.

Applications for modifications to existing home loans to some mortgage servicers must be initiated by home owners who currently occupy the home as their primary residence. Vacation homes do not qualify, nor does investment property.

This is not a hard a fast rule. Restrictions have been relaxed, making it possible to modify some homes that are held for investment purposes. The rules and guidelines that govern modifications are constantly changing, so be sure to tease out whether residency requirements are applicable or not from your mortgage servicer.

©Robert Rodgers, PhD

Stop Foreclosure

Regardless of the rules that apply to your circumstance it will always be to your advantage if the home in question is your primary residence. If it is investment property, you may still be able to apply but you will inevitably encounter a myriad of additional rules, regulations and restrictions.

What are the Two Most Important Considerations for Whether I Will Succeed in Getting My Mortgage Modified to a Lower Payment?

Two considerations determine for the most part whether you will succeed in obtaining a modification to your home loan which makes it possible to pay a lower mortgage payment each month.

> **1. How much equity do you currently have in your home?**
>
> **2. Do you have sufficient income that is sustainable?**

Determination of Equity in Your Home

The most significant factor that determines whether you will succeed with getting a loan modification is the current equity in your home.

©Robert Rodgers, PhD

Stop Foreclosure

By equity I mean the difference between what your home is likely to sell for in the marketplace today minus the amount of all liens against the property (including a first mortgage, Lines of Credit (LOL) and all other second or third liens against the property). If you have been paying a mortgage for several decades, you will probably have a sizable equity in your home unless you have refinanced your home one or several times since the original purchase.

Keep in mind that your equity is based on the marketplace, not on the price you paid for the home when you originally purchased it. If the market prices of homes in your neighborhood have dipped well below the price you paid for you home originally (as was the case for many individuals in 2009-2012) your current equity will have shrunk significantly. For some people, their equity has vanished entirely. Others are in the hole so to speak. They owe more on their home that it is worth in the marketplace today.

Get a firm handle on the total debt you owe today on your home. This will include the primary or first mortgage, any second mortgages, lines of credit

©Robert Rodgers, PhD

Stop Foreclosure

and any liens that might have been placed on the property for improvements or repairs that were done on the property but remain unpaid.

How do you figure the current market value? Banks employ appraisal companies who collect data on the sales of houses just like yours in your neighborhood. If there are no houses exactly like yours (which is the case under normal circumstances) appraisers identify houses that are as close as possible to your home with regard to the square footage, number of bedrooms and baths and lot size that have sold within the past six months.

Because the houses they have selected as comparable homes have sold, appraisers already know their value as was recently determined by a marketplace sale. Because the houses are not precisely like your home, they will then enter adjustments to estimate the market value of your house if it were sold today.

Adjusters will increase the value of a house that was sold for features that your house has that the comparable house lacks and decrease the value

Stop Foreclosure

for features that your house lacks that the comparable houses has. Allow me to take just one simple example.

One of the three comparable homes that the adjuster identified sold for $200,000. It had three bedrooms. Your home has four bedrooms and 200 square feet more than the comparable house. Because your house is a little larger in terms of square feet and has one more bedroom, it is assumed that it would have sold for more money. The adjuster then adds an increment to adjust for the increased value of your home relative to the home that actually sold. Adjustments are of course rather arbitrary, but it would not be unreasonable for an adjuster to add $3,500, making the total value of this house to be 203,500 in order for it to be comparable to your home. This then is the figure that would be averaged with the other two comparable homes that sold to estimate the market value of your home,

The same analysis is done for the other two comparable homes. If the comparable home is smaller or has fewer features, the price it sold for will be reduced by an increment determined by

©Robert Rodgers, PhD

Stop Foreclosure

the appraiser. They tend to use boilerplate figures for adjustments which are all of course simply good guesses. No one knows what your house will sell for if placed on the market today.

In summary, three (3) homes determined by an appraiser to be comparable to your home in terms of location and size are typically used to determine the fair market value of your house. Once the adjustments are made to the houses that sold (with increases for features that your house has that the comparable house lacks and decreases for features that your house lacks that the comparable houses have), the three values of comparable homes are averaged. This becomes the market value of your house that the mortgage companies use to determine whether it advantageous to them to modify your loan at a lower mortgage.

The analysis may appear to be technical and scientific, but I can assure you that it is entirely arbitrary. Often, the comparable units are selected by an appraiser who knows nothing about your neighborhood. They may select homes in a neighborhood where prices of homes are

Stop Foreclosure

double that of the prices of homes in your neighborhood. Selection of properties that are comparable to yours and used to determine the market value of your home is always up for discussion and challenge.

Be sure to keep close track of the price of homes in your neighborhood that have sold recently. You can perform your own market analysis and get a good idea of the fair market value of your own home. When it comes to getting a loan modification, you will want the value of your home to be as small as possible. Negative equity would be most desirable!

If the appraisal makes your home appear to have a higher value than is accurate, be sure to challenge it! All market appraisals are arbitrary. Any and all aspects of any appraisal can be challenged – including such factors as the selection of the comparable homes, the size of adjustments that were made or the description of the features found in your own home, etc.

©Robert Rodgers, PhD

Stop Foreclosure

Little or No Equity Is Preferable When It Comes to Modifying Your Loan

A small or nonexistent equity is welcome news when it comes to securing a loan modification.

The more the equity in your home, the less likely it is that you will succeed in securing a home modification.

Having a big chunk of equity is a bad thing when it comes to getting a lender to modify your loan. I suspect you are thinking I must have this backwards, right? After all, haven't you demonstrated a good faith effort to make payments on your home until now, when a recent, unfortunate circumstance has made it impossible to make your monthly mortgage payment? Of course you have, but that does not make a bit of difference to the banks. All they care about is your ability to pay today, not yesterday.

As financial institutions, banks are not moved or persuaded by your personal circumstances.

You have been screwed by your employer?

The financial institutions don't care.

©Robert Rodgers, PhD

Stop Foreclosure

You have a legitimate law suit against your employer which your lawyer says you will win?

The financial institutions don't care.

You were in a horrible accident which put you out of work for months?

The financial institutions don't care.

They are financial institutions. They were incorporated to make money. They are not social service organizations supported by foundations or governments. Do not think for a moment that they will be persuaded by your story of hardship and angst.

Their position is that you signed an agreement to put your home up as collateral for a home loan. The agreement states that if you fail to make payments as specified in the loan agreement, the lending entity has a right to siege your property through a foreclosure proceeding.

The financial institutions (usually banks) evaluate the benefit of foreclosing on your home when compared to the benefit of offering you a modification to your existing loan at a lower

©Robert Rodgers, PhD

Stop Foreclosure

interest rate. The decision to offer a modification is purely a financial decision. They do not care what benefits you and they have no obligation to offer a modification. When I say benefit here – I am talking dollars and cents.

In more technical terms, their evaluation considers whether the net present value of the income stream from the modified loan exceeds expected foreclosure sale proceeds. Any Federal HAMP loan requires that a Net Present Value calculation be performed. If the home owner passes the NPV test, they are technically qualified for a modification. I will explain in the next sections the various factors (or variables) that must be entered into the NPV calculation.

I encourage you to perform your own NPV. If have little or no equity in your home but you do now have a source of regular income the Net Present Value Test will pass and you will technically be qualified for a modification.

Be forewarned however that the mortgage servicing companies do not use the NPV to decide whether to offer you a modification. They will run through the calculations only because the HAMP

Stop Foreclosure

program requires that a home owner will not qualify for a HAMP loan if they do not pass the NPV test. I have served as a mediator in many foreclosure mediations where the mortgage servicing company is reluctant to show the results of a NPV or even discuss the inputs they used to determine whether the home owner passes (and thus qualifies for a modification) or fails (and thus do not qualify).

The critical consideration is this:

Does the investor get more money from modifying your loan than it will get from foreclosing?

If the mortgage servicing company can make more money by foreclosing on your home rather than offering you a loan modification, they will foreclose. Unless you can pay off all of the past due amounts in arrays, you will face a foreclosure on your home. It does not matter how compelling the reason might be that you have documented for the delinquency.

Estimates are that it costs an average of $125,000 to foreclose on a property so the financial

©Robert Rodgers, PhD

Stop Foreclosure

institutions prefer to avoid foreclosure in most cases. OF course, these figures are highly confidential and will vary considerably across situations and states. The difficulty with obtaining a modification skyrockets in situations where equity in the home is sizeable.

For example, let us say that the difference between the appraised market value of your home less all the debt is $195,000. Your equity is $195,000. Because it costs less than $195,000 to foreclose, there will likely be a compelling hesitancy to even consider the possibility of a loan modification. Too much profit can be made by resorting to a foreclosure.

The $125,000 cost of a foreclosure is only a gross estimate. The actual figure for some cases may be half that amount or less. However, the final cost of foreclosing on a property is typically a lot higher than most people realize. It also takes a lot longer as well. So, both time and the costs of foreclosure are to your advantage. Your mortgage servicer would much prefer to avoid a foreclosure if they can service the debt with new payments

©Robert Rodgers, PhD

Stop Foreclosure

you make, even if the payments are considerably less than under the original plan.

If you do happen to have a sizeable equity in your home I recommend that you put your home up for sale now. The bank will see that it is much more advantageous to foreclose than to offer you a loan modification. Recoup the equity for yourself rather than giving it all to the bank. The average time for a foreclosure sale is a year to a year and a half, so you have time on your side to find a buyer. The bank will be happy with that outcome as well.

If you sell your home for a price that does not cover all of the debt owed, you will likely still incur a debt to the mortgage company for the amount of debt that is not repaid. It is best to sell your home for a price that covers all of the debt that is owed plus the closing expenses. If you have to leave your home, you do not also want to incur an ongoing debt.

We had no equity in our home after refinancing several times over a five year period. Market values had dropped significantly in our neighborhood since we purchased our home

©Robert Rodgers, PhD

Stop Foreclosure

which we love. If the bank had foreclosed on us and attempted to sell the property, they would have incurred a significant loss. This was all to our advantage. It was the primary reason they were willing to extend a modification at a much lower interest rate. My success had nothing to do with the reason I provided for the hardship or the fact that I am a nice guy.

I am Currently Unemployed and Have No Prospects of a Job. What are My Chances of Getting My Home Loan Modified?

I have to be the source of bad news, but you have no chance of getting your home loan modified if you do not have any income at this time. Even if you do land a good job, you will have to show three months of income from your job before your new situation will count in evaluating your application for a modification.

Now if you expect to be employed soon I suggest that you apply for a modification to slow the foreclosure process down. Expect that your application will be denied. You will incur additional penalties and late fees, but the costs may be worth it to keep your home. You would

Stop Foreclosure

not want to expedite the review process, so there is no rush in FAXING the information that is requested.

Alternatively, get serious about selling your home. It really may be your best option and may even provide a cushion to help you and your family sail through the difficult circumstances you currently face.

What Hit on My Credit Rating Will I Take For Not Making My Mortgage Payments?

What I learned since taking the hit on my credit rating when I was in the midst of seeking a modification was the following. Failure to pay a mortgage results initially in a large reduction in your credit rating – a much as 100 points. However, once you begin making payments on a regular and timely basis again, your credit rating will be restored relatively quickly. My rating jumped back to its original level within a year after we began making regular and timely payments again under the modified arrangement.

©Robert Rodgers, PhD

Stop Foreclosure

What Documentation Will I Be Required to Produce?

Although the specific documentation that will be required by various lenders varies, all home owners are in general required to provide the following:

1. Documentation of any and all current streams of ongoing income that are received. One time payments do not enter into the equation here unless they are tied to your business. If you are self-employed, the last three profit and loss statements will be required.

2. Documentation on income received over the past three months through submission of bank statements or pay stubs

3. Statement of all other debts and obligations (credit card debt, car payments and all other installment debts which are obligatory).

4. Tax returns for the past two years. In most cases, you will be asked to sign a form that

Stop Foreclosure

gives the mortgage servicing company the right to request your last two years of tax filings from the IRS. You typically do not copy and FAX these documents yourself (though it may be required).

Let's now get down to specifics. As a general rule most mortgage servicers require the home owner to FAX detailed documentation of the hardship involved and current income. I have not even addressed the specifics of what you will have to submit!

As you can readily see from the specifics of the requirements listed below, it can be a genuine hardship in itself to produce all of the documentation needed to complete a modification application. I can assure you that if you do not send the documentation required to support a claim of income, your application will not even be reviewed.

To apply for a modification to your home mortgage you will be required to submit the following documentation:

©Robert Rodgers, PhD

Stop Foreclosure

- Completed and signed financial and hardship affidavit statement is obligatory.

- Copies of most recent pay stubs for the past three months must be faxed (if applicable).

- Documented proof is required for all sources of secondary or additional income.

- Written verifications are required from the sources of all other earned income including bonuses, commissions, fees, housing allowances, tips and/or overtime.

- If self-employed, a profit and loss statement must be submitted for a minimum of the last three months documenting all income received and expenses incurred.

- Documentation of all benefit income from social security, disability, death benefits and/or pension income must be submitted from the provider of the benefit specifying the amount and frequency of the benefit. In addition, copies of two most recent bank statements showing the deposits must also be submitted. Bank statements cannot be more than 90 days old.

©Robert Rodgers, PhD

Stop Foreclosure

- Documentation of alimony or child support must be provided in the form of a copy of the divorce decree, separation agreement or other legal written document showing the amount of the award and the time period over which it will be received. In addition, copies of two most recent bank statements must be provided showing deposits in the amounts specified in the legal agreements. Again, bank statement must not be over 90 days old.

- If you are declaring rental income you must submit a copy of your most recent federal tax return including Schedule E (Supplemental Income) and a copy of the rental or lease agreement.

- If you are declaring unemployment benefits, you must submit a copy of the benefits statement or official letter from the provider stating the amount, frequency and duration of the benefit. In addition, copies of the two most recent bank statements or other documentation showing receipt of the benefit. (Again, bank statements must not be over 90 days old).

©Robert Rodgers, PhD

Stop Foreclosure

- If you are declaring additional income from any source, you must provide a signed and dated letter from the person (s) contributing the income showing its amount, frequency and intended duration. This includes, for example, a situation where you rent out a room in your home to another person.

- You must submit a signed and dated copy of IRS Form 4506T-EZ – a Request for Transcript of Tax Return with all applicable fields completed for each borrower on the mortgage note. This form is required even if you have not filed a tax return or are not required to file one. This gives the servicer the authority to request a copy of your tax returns from the IRS.

- You must submit a copy of a utility, phone or cable bill to validate current occupancy.

Why Do I Have to Keep Re-Submitting the Same Documentation?

Almost everyone who applies for a modification is shocked to discover how long the application process takes. Why is that? All of the documentation must be recent. This means each

Stop Foreclosure

and every document you have submitted must be dated within the most recent 90 period. Most applicants discover that they are required to re-submit documentation over and over again because one or more of the documents are outdated or missing. It can easily take three months just to submit all of the documentation which is required for a review of your request for a modification. In the usual circumstance documents submitted early often become outdated by the time all documents have been received.

Suppose one of the bank statements you FAXED two months ago to support your receipt of disability income is now 80 days old. This is within the 90 day limit. Your application is complete and submitted for review and consideration. You figure you are good to go with a decision which you fully expect will be favorable.

I am afraid not my friend. Why? The review process takes 15 days. In fifteen days after submitting your application for review, the documentation on your disability becomes

©Robert Rodgers, PhD

Stop Foreclosure

outdated by five days. What is the likely decision to be?

A rejection! You will likely receive a form letter stating that your application has been denied because your information is not current. Of course, it is highly unlikely you will be informed which of the documents in particular is outdated, but it is possible that a phone representative might be able to determine this for you. If you are keeping close track of the dates on all of your documents you will know the answer yourself without even having to ask.

What is your recourse? Initiate a fresh application immediately. To be sure, this setback is totally frustrating and usually a shock to a home owner. Much of the documentation you previously submitted now has to be updated. At least one bank statement is going to be over 90 days old. Letters written about the sources of additional income will likely have to be updated and signed a second time with more recent date stamps. New pay stubs or more recent profit and loss statements (if you are self-employed) will have to

Stop Foreclosure

be updated and FAXED. In short, all of the documentation has to be re-done.

Has this already happened to you? I would venture a guess yes if you have already applied for a modification. Know that you are not alone. This is the experience most people encounter.

What can you do to avoid the frustration of delays and demands for updated documents? Keep a watchful eye on the dates of all documents you have submitted for review. Let your servicer know that you know when the documents expire. Call them every other day after your application is complete and has been submitted for review. Make the following request to the phone representative each time you call them (which I recommend should be every other day):

> *Thank you for submitting my application for review. As you are well aware, one of my documents (state which one) is dated (state the date). This document will be over 90 days old within (state the number of days). Please make a decision by (state the date) so that my all of my documents will fall within the 90 day period.*

©Robert Rodgers, PhD

Stop Foreclosure

I am not walking away from my commitment. This modification is important for me and my family. Please make a note of my request in the file. (Confirm this has been done before you hang up).

This lets the servicer know that you know the rules and that you expect an expeditious decision. Keep in mind that it is to the advantage of the servicer to stall the process because they collect more penalty and late fees the longer the process takes. Make an extra effort to make these delaying tactics a little more difficult.

Just because you request an expeditious review does not mean you will get one, but try anyway. Now, if a document expires before a decision on your modification is made (and you know which document is outdated because you are tracking dates on all the documents), FAX an updated document to the servicer before it becomes outdated. Call the servicer and verify they received it.
This will prevent a rejection form letter that states you were denied because your documents were outdated.

©Robert Rodgers, PhD

Stop Foreclosure

Some people do not like to call frequently. This is primarily because these calls can be so unpleasant. You will always be pestered to make a payment. You will usually be treated with disrespect. The phone representative will tell you that the review of your application takes 15 days and you will receive a decision in the mail.

Call anyway at least 3 or 4 times a week. The process of getting your loan modified is not about proving to yourself or the servicer how nice and patient of a person you are. Your objective by making the calls is to make it crystal clear that you have done your homework and know that you should be qualified to get your loan modified. Always request that the phone representative make a note in your file that you called and summarize what you said.

How Much Income Must I Show to Qualify for a Modification?

If you have no income, you will not succeed with obtaining a loan modification. Generally speaking the banks like to see that the mortgage payment you are able to make is at least 31% of your gross monthly income. The term gross income means

Stop Foreclosure

the total amount of money you and your co-borrower earn.

As noted, mortgage servicers require that you provide at least three months evidence of all income that you claim to be receiving. Bank statements are typically required that show evidence of income if employed by someone else.

If you are self-employed and have your own business at least three months profit and loss statements are required. You must prepare these statements and verify the authenticity of the statement. No additional verifications are required other than the profit and loss statement that you prepare and FAX to the servicer. The servicer typically will not ask to see statements of your business bank account to verify your income flow.

You can claim income from any source – a second job, income from relatives, income from the rental of other properties, etc. – but any income you claim must be documented. You will want this figure to be as high as possible, so be sure and claim income from any source that is ongoing and

Stop Foreclosure

that will add to the total monthly income you can claim.

If a relative gives you cash every month, be sure to deposit it into a bank account rather than spend it outright. That way there will be clear documentation that you receive that income each and every month. Most mortgage companies require that you document only the most recent three months of activity.

Suppose you just came into an installment source of revenue through a retirement fund that just kicked in, or you just started receiving social security. You can show proof of the first month's deposit into your bank account. If you are serious about claiming this new source of income, you will have to wait an additional month before a decision can be made on your application. You will need to show evidence of at least two months of social security (or disability) deposits. One deposit is insufficient.

Can I Protect my Savings, IRAS and Health Savings Accounts?

Your monthly income has tanked. You are struggling to pay your grocery bills and keep the

Stop Foreclosure

electricity turned on because there is little or no stream of current income. But, you do have a safety net: a modest savings account that you have been building up over the years for a rainy day just like today. What is the chance you can protect your savings and still succeed with obtaining a modification to your mortgage? Obviously, every situation is different, but what are the odds?

Very slim indeed. Why? The mortgage servicing company will see that you have a reserve of funds. Their position is this: If you want to keep your home, then dip into your savings and keep your mortgage current. They will wait you out. They will harass you. I suspect in most cases, people who want to stay in their homes will fold and dip into their savings until a current stream of income is found.

People have invented many ways to hide such reserves. They transfer the savings to a family member for example. The reality is that such manipulations are usually detected by the mortgage servicing companies. They will require

Stop Foreclosure

bank statements and see if there was a large transfer of funds out of your account recently.

I would recommend that you plan on using whatever funds you have available to cover your mortgage until the funds are exhausted (if you want to keep your home). Let your mortgage servicing company know that you have now spent every last penny in your savings accounts and are now bone dry. This makes a compelling case that supports your intention to meet your payment commitments as long as they can be reduced to a more affordable level.

What are My Chances for Getting My Mortgage Loan Modified If I Currently Have No Income as I Just Lost My Job, but am Certain I Will Land Gainful Employment Soon?

Promises and/or high expectations have a strong influence in the final decision to grant a modification. They will insure that your application will be denied because you have no income. Period.

If you have no current income but expect to land a good job soon I suggest that you find some way to

Stop Foreclosure

cover the mortgage if you can. Credit cards can be helpful in this regard, as can family and friends. Do not expect a warm reception to defer your payments while you look for another job. If you have no income you will not qualify for a modification.

If you cannot cover the payments, you might consider applying for a modification as a stalling tactic. Once you land your new job, you can negotiate a higher payment which amortizes the late fees, penalties and payments you missed. If your salary will not justify the higher payment, then you might well be in a strong position to qualify for a modification at a lower rate.

I Just Landed A Good Job. Why was My Application for a Modification to My Mortgage Denied?

You have to show three monthly of income before the income counts in the calculations. If you just started your new job you will not be able to show evidence that you have received three months of salary. You will probably be told that you can always re-apply, but that your modification has been denied. The case will be closed and the

Stop Foreclosure

process of foreclosing on your property will move forward.

This will sound scary and ridiculous I know. Take a deep breath. Realize that it takes at least 90 days to foreclose on a property in most states (although laws in some states are expediting the foreclosure process). Always keep in mind that the mortgage companies want the money, not the property! They are not going to hurry up a foreclosure process when there is a good chance they may be able to capitalize on three more months of late fees and penalties and that you are now in a position to make payments.

If you are calling every other day, you will hear word of the denial weeks before you receive the written form letter notice in the snail mail. Take positive action the same day you hear about the denial when you call.

FAX a written letter to your mortgage company explaining that you are now employed. Include a copy of your job offer. Explain that you will re-apply for a modification after you can show evidence that three months of salary have been

Stop Foreclosure

deposited into your bank account. Call the next day to confirm the FAXES were received.

Send follow-up FAXES updating your situation every time you receive income from your job. And of course, always call the following day to verify that your FAX was received. Keep a record of the name of the phone representative you talk with each time you call along with the date and time of the call. FAX a copy of each bank statement that shows a salary deposit (without including your bank account number).

When you initiate a new application for a modification, FAX the bank statements from three most recent months that show clear evidence of salary deposits. Do not assume that your mortgage servicer will have this evidence even though you have FAXED it earlier. These computer files can become quite unwieldy, making it difficult for managers to locate information that you might have FAXED months ago. Take nothing for granted when corresponding with your servicer.

©Robert Rodgers, PhD

Stop Foreclosure

What Mortgage Payment Can I Qualify For?

Your front end Debt-to-Income Ratio (DTI Ratio) is used by mortgage servicing companies to determine whether a homeowner's monthly mortgage payment is "affordable." The front end Debt to Income (DTI) ratio is calculated by dividing homeowner's current monthly mortgage payment by homeowner's gross monthly income. The current percent that is expected is 31%.

A second ratio that is factored into the decision is known as the Back-End Ratio. This ratio is calculated by taking the payment required under a modified mortgage loan plus all reoccurring monthly expenses divided by the home owner's total income. The back end ratio should not exceed 55%.

How can you calculate whether you might qualify for a modification? Sum up income from all sources that you receive on an ongoing basis each month. Then, take 31% of this amount. For example, if you earn $3,000 a month from all sources, calculate 31% of this amount (3,000 x .31 = 930) which is $930. This amount ($930) is the monthly mortgage payment that a mortgage

Stop Foreclosure

company will technically qualify you for. Taxes and insurance are usually not factored into this analysis.

The 31% figure is not set in concrete. It does change from time to time. The Front End Debt to Income Ratio used to be as high as 36% a short decade ago. Your mortgage servicing company may apply a figure that is slightly different from 31%. The thirty-one percent baseline is the norm at this time for most financial institutions.

If your mortgage company modifies your loan, they want to be in a position to bundle it up with other mortgages and sell it off to another institution. Many potential buyers are actually government programs like Fannie Mae and Freddie Mac. They hold beneficiaries to a strict set of lending standards (which change often). If your debt to income ratio is more than 31% (or .31) your loan will be difficult to "unload" or sell to another investor which is the name of the game these days.

If you do not pass the Back End DBI Ratio test, you may also be disqualified, but you never know. Willingness to modify a loan hinges on a variety of

Stop Foreclosure

factors and circumstances. It is to your advantage if sales of homes in your neighborhood are depressed and to your disadvantage if sales are booming.

Is the 31% rule hard and fast? If the modification is through a government sponsored program, the answer is yes. Many loan modifications these days however are "in house" modifications which simply means that the mortgage servicer extends whatever offer they wish under whatever terms suits their fancy. The mortgage servicing company is not bound to honor the 31% cut off particularly when it comes to offering an in house modification.

Will it be to the lender's advantage to offer you the terms of a modified agreement that lowers your monthly payment? As noted, your mortgage company will likely be receptive to offering a modification to your existing loan when there is little or no equity in the home. They will also be more willing to extend a modification offer if they are convinced that you will meet your commitment to pay the new, lower mortgage every month.

©Robert Rodgers, PhD

Stop Foreclosure

Guidelines for Reporting Expenses

In addition to asking for an accounting of your expenses, your application for a modification also requires that you disclosure your monthly expenses. As a general rule, you want the total expenses to be as little as possible within reason. If you claim an expense that is too high or low, the mortgage servicer will usually question it. You will not be required to document your expenses however as is the case with income.

Mortgage servicers use certain private and unpublished guidelines that specify the average monthly expenses that are allowable for food, transportation, medical expenses, insurance, etc. depending on the number of persons in the family. If it appears as though spending patterns are out of the range of average consumers, your mortgage servicer may suggest that you should be able to pay your existing mortgage by cutting all unnecessary and extravagant expenses.

I have mediated foreclosure mediations where the mortgage servicer manager with authority to make a modification decision asked the home owner to examine any and all expenses that could

Stop Foreclosure

be reduced or eliminated. This increased their net income and made the modification of a loan more appealing. Always keep in mind that mortgage loans are bought and sold all the time. There is always an incentive to a mortgage servicer to make your financial situation appear as strong as possible.

As a general rule, it is advisable to exclude any expenses that are not essential. For example, you may be paying $150 a month for cable TV. Is that expense essential? Obviously not. Do not report it. If necessary to meet your mortgage payment, you could always eliminate cable TV for a spell. Check out movies from the library for free instead.

From my experience as a mediator, the expense side of the equation is not as critical as the income side. If you are a little light on the income side of the equation, consider some options that will make it easier to get a modification.

Get a part time job for three months before you apply for a modification. That additional income can be added to your total. This will make a favorable decision much more likely. After you have succeeded in getting you loan modified, you

Stop Foreclosure

have no obligation to continue working at the part time job (unless necessary to meet your monthly payment).

What are the Most Common Reasons for Requesting a Modification?

The banks want to see that the hardship reason you have been unable to pay your mortgage is temporary. If the reason is not temporary, they will have no reason to expect that your future ability to pay will be any different from your previous inability to pay.

- *Did you lose your job and are looking for another? Great. That is a good reason.*

- *Did you recently get divorced and were required to pay out bundles of money to your spouse? Great. That is a good reason. The financial hit will pass with time.*

- *Did you or your family have health problems which drained the family budget? That is not great for you and your family but that too is a good reason. Health problems typically resolve with time and proper treatment.*

©Robert Rodgers, PhD

Stop Foreclosure

- *Are you guilty of poor financial planning? You simply had not entered an expense into your budget which was not properly anticipated or even known? This is not a great reason, but it may suffice.*

In other words, if it seems to the mortgage company that your current hardship will resolve in time, you have a solid reason for requesting a modification.

According to Freddy Mac, job loss is the number one reason for requesting a modification top the terms of a home loan. A survey from 2010 revealed the frequency of reasons for requesting a modification:

Reason for the Hardship	Per Cent
Unemployment or curtailment of income	55
Excessive obligation	29
Illness or death in the family	8
Marital difficulties	4
Inability to sell or rent property	2
Employment transfer or military	1

©Robert Rodgers, PhD

Who Are the Players When It Comes to Getting My Mortgage Modified?

1. Mortgage originator
2. Mortgage holder
3. Mortgage servicer
4. Lender's attorney

When you buy a home and sign a mortgage or deed of trust you are working with the mortgage originator. You may think that the originator will hold and service your loan until you pay it off or sell your home. This is what happened several decades ago. The mortgage instrument was stored in the bank's safe.

That is seldom the case these days. In today's mortgage market, loans (and the rights to service them) are bought and sold on an open market as if they were stocks trading on the New York Stock Exchange.

The mortgage servicer that you send your payment to is not the financial institution that originated your loan or owns your loan. They are

Stop Foreclosure

called a servicer because that is their role: they send out monthly statements, collect payments and deal with defaults.

You may be paying your loan to Chase or Wells Fargo or Bank America. It may appear as though these institutions own your mortgage note because they are financial institutions. The institution you make your payment to has a servicing agreement to administer your loan with the institution that owns it. They collect payments from you, assess late charges (which they retain), chase after you if you fail to make your payment on time and handle all loan modifications.

Many people have the incorrect belief that the bank (or mortgage servicing company) that they pay their mortgage to is the institution that holds or owns the mortgage. This can be the case in very rare and special circumstances but more often than not the company that you must deal with in requesting a modification of the loan is a company which has been contracted to service the loan. They do not own the mortgage note on property. These agreements between the beneficiary (who

Stop Foreclosure

owns your mortgage note) and the servicer are better known as servicing agreements.

Your loan has been bundled together with a group of other loans. The servicing agreement which applies to your loan is an agreement that applies to all loans in that particular bundle which includes your loan.

Servicing agreements are technical. Even lawyers have very different interpretations of the meaning behind some of the language that is found. As a general rule servicing agreements require that the mortgage servicing company convey any and all payments for mortgages to whatever institution is the holder (or owner) of your the mortgage note.

Who holds (or owns) your mortgage note? As noted, it is highly unlikely that the bank that initiated your note holds (or owns) the note now. You have probably heard of Fannie Mae and Freddie. They are government entities that purchase approximately 50% of all home mortgage loans. These two institutions were established by the government to make more loans available.

©Robert Rodgers, PhD

Stop Foreclosure

Holders of the mortgage deeds also reside with insurance companies, trust funds, retirement companies, union pension funds as well as savings and loan institutions. The originator of the loan is typically a bank but they do not hold onto the note.

The servicing companies are paid a fee to collect the payments. They also benefit directly from all late charges and other fees depending on the agreement with the institution that owns your mortgage lien.

You may think that you know who owns your mortgage. Why? Because you can look at the original documents and see who is listed as the beneficiary. Your mortgage note has probably been sold off to other institutions several times over. It is often difficult to determine who holds your mortgage since it is rarely the institution that originally funded the loan. Ownership may change hands many times.

The current institutions who own or hold your mortgage note executed a servicing agreement with the institution that you are required to send your mortgage payments to. The agreements vary

©Robert Rodgers, PhD

Stop Foreclosure

of course, but most of the agreements convey all of the late fees and service fees directly to the servicing company. This means that the institution you are dealing with for a modification actually benefits from all late fees that you have incurred because of a loan default.

It is to the advantage of the mortgage servicer to delay the process of modifying the loan because late fees and penalties are assessed with each passing month.

Even when a property is foreclosed, the mortgage servicer typically receives all the funds they have charged you in late charges and penalties off the top (from the sale proceeds) before any settlement is paid to the holders of the lien. It is to their advantage to stall a modification decision or foreclosure as long as possible? You betcha.

How Can I Determine Who Services My Home Mortgage and Who Owns My Mortgage Note?

The easiest way is to identify the company that services your mortgage is to examine the mortgage statements you receive in the mail each month. You may question whether the company

Stop Foreclosure

listed on the statement is actually authorized to service your loan (or if the statement is a scam or a fraud).

You can verify the name of the company that is authorized to service your loan by visiting the MERS website:

http://www.mers-servicerid.org

In addition, your mortgage servicer (the company you mail your payments to) must, upon written request, provide the borrower (who is you – the home owner) with the name and contact details for the owner of your mortgage note. You can also obtain information on the owner of the note through the MERS website listed above.

When I conducted the MERS search on my home address I learned that Bank of America is the company that services my mortgage loan. This is not the name of the financial institution that I forward my payments to. Bank of America has contracted with another company to handle all of the servicing on my loan. You may be surprised to learn who is really responsible for servicing your loan.

©Robert Rodgers, PhD

Stop Foreclosure

My Mortgage Servicer Tells Me that the Owner of My Note is Different from What I see on my Original Mortgage Note. Can This Be True?

Yes. Most people are surprised by how many times the holder of their mortgage note has changed hands. I have even heard of an instance where the institution that holds the note changed hands three times since a request for mediation was submitted. We are talking here only three months! In other words, the note changed ownership every month. The current owner should be listed on the MERS website.

Can I Determine who Owns My Mortgage Note By Searching Deeds of Trust Filed with My County Courthouse?

Each time a mortgage note changed hands before MERS was established, a document had to be filed in the local county courthouse of the local jurisdiction where the home was located. The filing of each document was accompanied by a filing fee. Now the courthouse documents list MERS as the holder of your mortgage note. No notification now needs to be recorded in country

Stop Foreclosure

courthouses when mortgage notes change hands. You will probably not find any evidence of who actually owns your mortgage note by searching the records that have been filed at your county court house.

What is MERS?

MERS stands for Mortgage Electronic Registration Systems Inc. It was founded in 1997 by twenty-three (23) mortgage giants including Bank of America, Fannie Mae, Freddie Mac and Wells Fargo for the purpose of centralizing and economizing the tracking of mortgages. As financial institutions began to trade bundles of mortgages on the fast paced financial market of the late 1990's they needed an efficient means of recording those transfers.

More than three thousand lenders have registered more than sixty-five million home mortgages with MERS since it was formed in 1997. When a lender/member of MERS originates a mortgage, the MERS name goes on the mortgage filed at the county courthouse because it is acting as the nominee or agent for the lender. When

Stop Foreclosure

your mortgage note is sold, you have to now contact MERS for the name of the new owner.

It became too costly, too time consuming and too inefficient to record transfers of paper documents at country courthouses each time a mortgage changed hands. When mortgages are sold now (which can be frequently) the lender does not have to file documents with the county court houses showing the transfer of ownership to another bank or investors in a trust.

With an electronic recording of transfers by MERS, the paper mortgage documents were either misplaced or shredded. While you may hold the original loan documents, there is a good chance that your mortgage servicer does not have the original loan note in their possession (nor is there any chance they could ever be located).

©Robert Rodgers, PhD

Stop Foreclosure

I Do Not Suspect that My Mortgage Servicing Company Has the Original Loan Documents. Why Can't I just Demand that They Produce the Original Documents? When They Can't Produce the Original Documents (as I Suspect) Doesn't My Loan Also Vanish and I Get My Home for Free?

Yes, it is certainly possible – perhaps even probable – that your mortgage servicing company does not have the original loan documents in their original paper form (the documents that you actually signed when you bought the home). The notes get sold and transferred so frequently that the original documents have been lost or even discarded in most instances.

And yes, there is a body of law that requires the original document of the mortgage or deed of trust be in the possession of the beneficiary (or financial institution) that owns the note. There are lawyers and companies that will be happy to take a case which argues the mortgage servicer does not own the note if they cannot produce it. Should you pursue this option?

©Robert Rodgers, PhD

Stop Foreclosure

Obviously, different people will offer different advice. I personally do not recommend this course of action for several reasons.

Let's say that your suspicion is correct and the mortgage loan documents cannot be produced. This actually is the usual case.

Some mortgage companies have falsified the original documents. While they lay claim to possessing them, the original documents no longer exist.

OK. So you get excited. The law is on your side. You decide to initiate a law suit to set aside the loan.

Unless I missed a critical detail, your personal financial situation is not exactly sound at the moment. How much money do you have to pay a lawyer to take your case? Can you trust this lawyer? As I see it, there is no way you will prevail. The law firms employed by the financial institutions always prevail in the end.

The bottom line is that you know and acknowledge to yourself that you agreed to accept a loan so you could take ownership of your

©Robert Rodgers, PhD

Stop Foreclosure

home. You agreed to pay that money back under certain terms and conditions that were agreeable to you at the time.

Yes, your circumstances have changed. You lost your job or have had health problems or …. But these recent, unfortunate circumstances do not negate the fact that you entered into a legally binding agreement. You got immediate ownership of your home in exchange for agreement to pay a monthly mortgage. You did not have to pay for the home in full before taking possession.

Instead of trying to get something for nothing, why not resign yourself to the reality that you need a little help digging out of a hole that you currently find yourself in? To make this happen you need your mortgage servicer's help to dig out of this hole. You can't do it alone. If you decide to sue your servicer, give up all hope of getting your loan modified to more favorable terms.

Should I Hire Someone Else to Handle My Application for a Mortgage Loan Application?

At this point, you are probably thinking it would be so much easier to hire someone else to handle

Stop Foreclosure

your modification request. The application process is so complicated and tedious. Right?

I have one short, succinct piece of advice for you. Do not do it.

Why? Most of the people and organizations that offer to process your application for a loan application are scams. Many extract large feeds from their clients and offer no palatable service in return. Reports of home owners who have been ripped off are plentiful.

Certainly there are a few reputable companies out there – but how can you tell who they are? I can't. Besides, it is much more compelling for a mortgage servicing company to hear directly from you, the home owner.

Think about it. You say you do not have the money to pay your mortgage, yet you are willing to pay someone am outrageous sum of money to help you lower your payment? Most of these companies do not even contact the mortgage company because they are scams. But even if they did, your mortgage servicer would surely become suspicious of the integrity of your claims that you

©Robert Rodgers, PhD

Stop Foreclosure

have insufficient resources to cover your mortgage.

Yes, it is a lot of trouble to apply for a loan modification. Yes, it takes a large chunk of time every week. But if you are serious about keeping your home, you are going to have to commit time, effort and energy into the process yourself. You can get assistance from housing counselors, but in the end, this is something you have to do yourself.

Is it really worth taking all the time and effort to process an application? If you actually figure out how much money you will save once a modification is finalized, you will be motivated to apply. Savings typically run into the hundreds of thousands of dollars. If you were going to be paid $1,000 an hour to do a job, would you apply for a modification today? There is no application fee!

Six Sure Signs of a Scam

1. A company/person asks for a fee in advance to work with your lender to modify, refinance or reinstate your mortgage.

©Robert Rodgers, PhD

Stop Foreclosure

2. A company/person guarantees they can stop a foreclosure or get your loan modified.

3. A company/person advises you to stop paying your mortgage company and pay them instead.

4. A company pressures you to sign over the deed to your home or sign any paperwork that you haven't had a chance to read, and you don't fully understand.

5. A company other than your lender claims to offer "government-approved" or "official government" loan modifications.

6. A company/person you don't know asks you to release personal financial information online or over the phone.

How Can I Avoid Being Scammed?

Now whatever course you decide to pursue, under no circumstances do the following:

- ***Do not sign over your deed of trust to someone who promises to sign it back over to you later.***

©Robert Rodgers, PhD

Stop Foreclosure

- *Do not pay a large fee up front to someone who promises to modify your loan.*

- *Do not give anyone direct access to your credit card or bank account.*

Why Did We Get a Foreclosure Notice when Our Mortgage Servicer was Still Evaluating Our Application for a Modification?

Ah – so this has happened to you? You were optimistic about a favorable decision on a modification and shocked that a registered notice of foreclosure was delivered to your home address which required your signature? This happens to many people.

Why does this happen? After all, the servicing company may well have instructed you not to make any payments until a decision was made on your application. "Do not worry", the phone representative told you the day before the letter arrived, "nothing will happen while your medication application is under review."

Stop Foreclosure

The mortgage servicing company (the institution you are dealing with to get a loan modification and the company where you send payments to) is an entirely different organization from the Trustee (typically a law firm) that is employed by the beneficiary (the investors who own your loan). The trustee is the entity that processes a foreclosure, not the mortgage servicer. You are not dealing with only one entity here!

The trustee may initiate foreclose proceedings regardless of the state of any modification that is in process. They represent the institution that owns your mortgage. It is often a case where the right hand has no idea what the left hand is doing nor does it care for that matter. The trustee may well not even know that a modification is being reviewed or considered by the servicer. And, they probably would not care anyway even if they knew.

The trustee likely has no information about what the servicing institution has told you or not told you. They have simply decided to initiate foreclose proceedings. Laws in most states state that a ninety day (90) waiting period is required

Stop Foreclosure

after a notification of foreclosure has been sent and acknowledged before any formal action of foreclosure can be initiated. The trustee wants to initiate the process as soon as possible regardless of the status of your application for a modification.

A streamlined version of foreclosures has recently been approved at the federal level, so the lengthy time required for most forecloses (which usually take well over a year and often two years) may soon be streamlined.

Why Do I have So Much Difficulty Dealing with My Mortgage Servicer?

Most financial institutions have insurance that guarantees they will be covered whether the loan defaults or not. In some cases, the government is the insurer. In other cases, the institutions actually have insurance policies that will cover the loan if you default. In such cases, they will not care a flip whether you can pay your mortgage or not. It is no skin off of their back. If a foreclosure sale nets less than the debt, the insurance will cover the difference.

©Robert Rodgers, PhD

Stop Foreclosure

Many mortgage institutions actually have hedge bets that you will be unable to make your payments. If you cannot make your payments, they still get paid. They win no matter what happens. They win regardless of the outcome of your ability to pay or the result of any modification that is offered.

What Happens When I Contact My Mortgage Servicer About Applying for a Modification?

All mortgage servicing company operate in the same fashion. You will never talk directly with anyone who has the authority to decide whether you qualify for a modification. Instead, the service representative who answers your call will be a minimum wage employee (often located in a foreign country) who is reading a set of instructions from their computer screen. Their primary job assignment is to pressure you for payment.

If you have submitted an application for a modification, they will read to you what appears on the computer screen that describes the current status of your application. They will usually tell

Stop Foreclosure

you that some documents are missing and must be faxed for your application to be reviewed. Or, you may be told that your documentation is complete and your application for a modification will be reviewed within 15 days. You will likely then be told that you will be notified in writing when a decision has been reached. It typically takes 10 to 15 days after a decision is reached for the notification to be received in the mail.

Each time you call for information about the status of your application you will be connected with a different customer service representative. Some companies do assign a single contact person, but this is rare. Each call will usually be unpleasant and unfriendly.

What Can I Expect when Calling My Mortgage Servicer?

It helps to stand in the shoes of the mortgage servicer as a way of better understanding why it is so difficult to deal with them. Some people who apply for a modification are using the process as a stalling tactic. They do not have the income that will justify a modification. Or, they may be confronted a variety of financial pressures that are

Stop Foreclosure

more pressing that paying their mortgage payment. They have discovered that they can get free rent so to speak for as long as a year to a year and a half if they simply stop making their payments.

Mortgage servicing companies are well aware of this tactic. It is rationale for them to put obstacles and barriers as a way of seeing how the home owner will react. The assessment is to see how serious the home owner really is with securing a modification and staying in their home. It is the custom to give you instructions to produce a document, then another document and then still another document.

Do you continue to produce the documents? Do you continue to comply with their requests? If so, you are probably serious about securing a modification and beginning to make payments again on a regular basis. If you are not responsive to these many requests, the mortgage company will have less trust that your application has been submitted in good faith.

The proportion of defaults once a temporary modification is offered is surprisingly high.

©Robert Rodgers, PhD

Stop Foreclosure

Servicers are hesitant to modify a loan (which is expensive in itself) if they suspect a home owner will default.

Below is a description of the typical experience of a home owner who is requesting a loan medication. For those of you who have already entered into the process, none of what I am about to describe will be unfamiliar.

1. You complete and FAX your application for a modification.
2. Several weeks pass. You have heard nothing back.
3. You call to ascertain the status of your application. You are told that a document is needed for your application can be submitted for a formal review. The requested documents are copies of the last three pay stubs. You are told that once they documents are received a formal review of your application for a modification will be initiated. This review will take 15 days to complete.
4. You FAX the documents the next day.
5. You wait 15 days as instructed.

©Robert Rodgers, PhD

Stop Foreclosure

6. You receive no notice in the mail.
7. You decide to call after waiting 20 days. You are told (by a different representative of course) that the documents were not received. You are told to re-submit the same documents. Once the pay stubs have been received your application will be submitted for a formal review and a decision made within 15 days.
8. You FAX the pay stubs the following day for a second time.
9. No notice is received in the mail.
10. You call after waiting 15 days. You are told that the pay stubs were received but that the bank statements you initially submitted are now out of date. All of the documents must be current and dated within the most recent three months. You must submit updated bank statements for your application to be submitted for a formal review. Once submitted, your application will be reviewed and you will be notified in writing (in a form letter) within 15 days.
11. You wait 15 days. No decision letter in the mail is received.

©Robert Rodgers, PhD

Stop Foreclosure

12. You call. You are told that the expenses you submitted appear to be higher than the average. You are instructed to re-evaluate the expenses you claimed and resubmit your application for review. The reviewer is also requesting verification of undocumented income you claimed from your spouse. You are told that once the additional documents are received your request will be reviewed and a decision made within 15 days. You are told to call back in 15 days.
13. You call back after a 15 day wait and are told that your bank statements and pay stubs are now out of date. You must provide the most recent three bank statements. One of your bank statements is 4 months old. You are told to update your bank statements. Once the documents have been received they will be submitted for review and further analysis. You will be notified in writing within 15 days after the application has been submitted.
14. You finally receive a written denial in the mail. The denial comes in the form a letter

Stop Foreclosure

with check boxes. One of the boxes is checked which says that you have been denied a HAMP modification. The rest of the form is difficult to read and impossible to understand. For all practical purposes it is gibberish. You have no more idea where you stand than when you first initiated the process a year ago and now you have been delinquent paying your mortgage for six months.

This is a simple preview of only the initial process of the application which continues on and on throughout the year with more and more documents that are requested. Often the documents that you FAXED were not received or at least the mortgage servicing company claims that the documents were not received.

This explanation is a streamlined version of what most people experience. What is really going on here? What can't the entire process be streamlined and simplified?

First, keep in mind that the servicing company has no incentive to deal with you in the first place. Each month you are late with you payments late

Stop Foreclosure

fees are charged. They are the beneficiary of these late fees. Remember that you are not dealing with the institution that loaned you the money – you are dealing with a company that has been contracted to service the loan. Any and all late charges and service fees are all paid off the top after any final resolution is reached (whether a modification, foreclosure, short sale or whatever). In other words, the servicing company is the sole beneficiary the longer it takes to reach a final decision.

Why Can't I Email the Documents to My Mortgage Servicer? It Would Be So Much Easier.

From my experience, most mortgage servicing companies require the application for a modification and all documents to be faxed and not emailed. It would be a good investment to set up a system for faxing documents from your home if you have not already done so. If you elect to FAX all of the documents from a business that provides FAX services, you will wind up paying a pretty penny before the ordeal is over. It would be highly unusual if you only had to FAX one set of documents once.

©Robert Rodgers, PhD

Stop Foreclosure

Why do mortgage servicers refuse to accept documents through email? There is a clear trace and date (and time) stamp of emails. The mortgage servicer can more easily claim that a faxed document was not received. Do not even try to email anything to your mortgage servicer. Your only option is to FAX and follow-up by a phone call to confirm receipt.

The reason most people do not like to call their servicer to get an updated status of their application is because the calls are so unpleasant. You will always be pressured to make a payment. The person has no knowledge of your case or your application. Do not let the unpleasantness discourage you from being aggressive. Simply explain that you have no intention of making any further payments until your application for a temporary modification has been approved.

What Can I Do to Hurry Up the Review Process and Get a Decision More Quickly? We have been Hassling with Our Mortgage Servicer Now for Over a Year

I will now offer important suggestions that I

Stop Foreclosure

believe may make a huge difference with your ability to succeed in obtaining a modification.

Call the Servicing Company Every Other Day

Take charge of the process. Ask for an update. If you FAXED materials – verify whether the documents were received. Record the date and time of the call in a journal. Include the name of the service representative you contacted. You will probably be given only their first name. Record whatever name they give you. Ask them to spell it unless the name is Bob or Tom.

If the service representative tells you that the documents you faxed yesterday were not received, FAX them again immediately. Call the following day to verify that the documents were received. If you get the same response, proceed to round three. Fax the documents again. Call the following day to verify.

If the documents were received you will be told (as always) to inquire after 15 days.

- *Tell the service representative that keeping your home is important to you.*

©Robert Rodgers, PhD

Stop Foreclosure

- *Tell them you will be calling for an update in two days.*

- *Tell them that you are not backing away from your commitment to pay the loan.*

- *Remind them you are requesting a lower, more affordable interest rate.*

- *Tell them your intention is to make good on your financial commitments including any and all late fees.*

- *Tell them that you wish to begin making mortgage payments under terms of the modification as soon as possible.*

Keep in mind that they are not the decision maker. They are an employee who is being paid a minimum wage.

Ask the phone representative to record on your file the fact that you called and requested an update and that you are committed to meeting your financial obligations but require a lower mortgage rate to do so

©Robert Rodgers, PhD

Stop Foreclosure

You will be pressured to make a partial payment or full payment. This will happen with every call you make to the mortgage servicer. Once again, be firm. Explain that you will not be making any further payments until your home loan has been modified. Every time you call make the same three points:

1. *The loan modification is extremely important to me. I want to keep my home.*

2. *I am not running away from my commitment to meet my monthly payments.*

3. *I will not make further payments until the loan has been modified.*

Every time you call, the service representative makes an entry into your record about the reason for your call. Always request that your concerns be entered into your record every time you call. The decision maker will see the record of repeated calls and be impressed with your determination and commitment to secure a modification.

©Robert Rodgers, PhD

Stop Foreclosure

Be consistent with the reason for your nonpayment

Every time you call, explain again the reason for your financial hardship. Be consistent and clear. Do not make the explanation confusing. If you say initially that you were robbed, then during a second call that your spouse became sick, the decision makers will become suspicious about your integrity. Both may be true, but it is far wiser to state one clear reason.

Keep in mind that some of the home owners that mortgage servicing companies deal with are scam artists and will lie at the drop of a hat. Explain that you are in a position to meet a lower monthly mortgage as long as the amount has been reduced to a level you can handle.

Ask to Speak to Manager

Laws in some states require that you have the right to speak directly to a manager who has decision authority instead of always speaking to the representatives who answers your call. Does your state have such a law? Perhaps so. Perhaps not.

©Robert Rodgers, PhD

Stop Foreclosure

Obviously you could research this and learn the answer. As a first step, I recommend that when talking to a phone representative on the phone that you ask to speak to a manager after you have submitted all of the documentation required for a review. Say simply:

> *"I understand it is my right to speak to a manager. I wish to exercise that right at this time."*

Whether your state has such a law or not, making this request sends a clear signal that you are serious about wishing to resume making payments on your mortgage at a lower, modified rate that is more affordable. If a law does exist in your state, you may actually succeed in having a conversation with a manager, but I would not hold your breath waiting for such a conversation!

I demanded the opportunity to talk with a manager. She did leave a message on my phone with her phone number. I called her back 20 different times, leaving a different message on her phone with each call. With each message I communicated my heart felt interest in obtaining a modification. I never talked with her but she

©Robert Rodgers, PhD

Stop Foreclosure

certainly got the message I was serious and committed.

How Exactly Can My Mortgage Be Modified to Reduce My Monthly Payments?

The configuration of your modified loan is not a negotiated arrangement. You do not have a face to face discussion about how the terms can be adjusted to meet your needs.

Always keep in mind that when you make you calls every other day to your mortgage servicer you are not talking with decisions makers. You will almost always be talking with clerks who are reading information off of computer screens. There are rare phone calls when you might actually be talking with a manager, but it is highly unlikely that you would know that they are a manager.

It is helpful to understand how loans can be adjusted to lower you monthly payment.

1. The interest rate can be lowered.
2. The term of the loan can be extended. For example, if your loan is currently set at 30

Stop Foreclosure

years, it can theoretically be reconfigured for 40 years.

3. Some of the principal can be forgiven. This option is rarely seen in practice.

4. The late fees and charges are set aside rather than folded into the total loan that you owe. When set aside, you will still be required to pay them off when the balance of the loan has been exhausted but you pay no interest on the amount due until the loan itself has been paid in full.

Mortgage servicers have programs that generate all possible combinations of interest rates and terms to generate various payment schemes. Since they have an idea of how much you, as the home owner, can pay based on the general rule of 31% of your gross income, it is possible to evaluate using a computer program whether any specific interest rate offered over a specific term is feasible in light of your current financial circumstances.

Payments are less when the term is extended and the interest rate is lowered. Mortgage servicers

Stop Foreclosure

generally prefer an arrangement which extends the term of the loan from, for example, 30 years to 40 years, but keeps the interest rate the same. This will lower the monthly payment, but increase their long term revenue stream.

Special Considerations for Loans in Default

If you fail to make one or more payments on your mortgage loan, your loan is in default. The servicer may then order "default-related services" to protect the value of the property. These services may include property inspections to make sure you are still living in the home and maintaining the property. If the property is not being properly maintained, the servicer may order "property preservation services," like lawn mowing, landscaping and repairing or boarding up broken windows and doors. The costs for these services, which can add up to hundreds or thousands of dollars, are charged to your loan account.

If the servicer starts to foreclose on your property, additional costs like attorney's fees, property title search fees, and other charges for mailing and

Stop Foreclosure

posting foreclosure notices will be charged to your loan account. That can add hundreds or thousands of dollars more to your loan, and make it even more difficult for you to bring the loan current and avoid foreclosure.

If you find yourself in this situation, stay in touch with your servicer. Servicers have different policies about when they will order default-related services. Some may not order property inspections or property preservation work if you let them know each month that you are still:

- *Living in the home*
- *Keeping it well maintained*
- *Working with them to resolve the default on your account*

Even so, it's important to review your billing statements carefully and question added fees. If fees appear on your statement under general headings like "other fees" or "corporate advances," contact your servicer – in writing – as soon as possible to get an explanation of those fees and a reason they've been charged to your account.

©Robert Rodgers, PhD

Stop Foreclosure

Am I Eligible to Apply for a Federal Making Home Affordable Modification?

When initially offered, the HAMP program eligibility required home owners to live in the home as their principal residence. This requirement was expanded in 2012 to permit a wider audience of home owners to participate. Those who can now apply under current rules are home owners who:

- Are applying for a modification on a home that is not their primary residence, but the property is currently rented or the homeowner intends to rent it.

- Previously did not qualify for HAMP because their debt-to-income ratio was 31% or lower.

- Previously received a HAMP trial period plan, but defaulted in their trial payments.

- Previously received a HAMP permanent modification, but defaulted in their payments, therefore losing good standing.

You may be eligible for HAMP if you meet all of the following criteria:

Stop Foreclosure

- You obtained your mortgage on or before January 1, 2009.

- You owe up to $729,750 on your primary residence or single unit rental property

- You owe up to $934,200 on a 2-unit rental property; $1,129,250 on a 3-unit rental property; or $1,403,400 on a 4-unit rental property

- The property has not been condemned

- You have a financial hardship and are either delinquent or in danger of falling behind on your mortgage payments (non-owner occupants must be delinquent in order to qualify).

- You have sufficient, documented income to support a modified payment.

- You must not have been convicted within the last 10 years of felony larceny, theft, fraud or forgery, money laundering or tax evasion, in connection with a mortgage or real estate transaction.

©Robert Rodgers, PhD

Stop Foreclosure

Will I Qualify for a Modification to My Home Loan that is Underwritten by the Federal HAMP Program?

The terms of the HAMP program are changing continuously, but the general idea is to provide temporary relief to a homeowner who is confronting transient financial difficulties. The payment is set at a much lower amount in the first year, only to rise each year thereafter for five years. Principal can also be deferred under certain circumstances, although deferral of principal is rare in most cases.

As a home owner you can determine for yourself whether you qualify for a HAMP modification before you even apply for review with your mortgage servicer. Knowing whether the result you calculate is positive or negative places you in a very advantageous bargaining position with your mortgage servicer.

Criteria specified to be met under the HAMP program (among others) is whether you pass or fail a Net Present Value (NPV) Test. What in the world is a NPV test? This is an analysis that shows whether it is more beneficial to the beneficiary (the owner of the mortgage) to modify the terms

Stop Foreclosure

of the current loan (which sets a lower monthly payment more affordable to the borrower) or foreclosure on the property.

If the Net Present Value (NPV) analysis shows that it is more beneficial to the beneficiary to foreclosure on your home, you will fail the test. If the analysis shows that it is more beneficial to modify the loan at a lower monthly payment you will pass the Net Present Value (NPV) test.

The final result is determined by the inputs that are entered. You need not defer to your mortgage servicer to perform the analysis while you wait for the end result. Do the analysis yourself using your own inputs. First, it helps to understand the reasoning behind Net Present Value Analysis.

Net Present Value Analysis

While the Net Present Value analysis may appear to be scientifically and technically accurate, it is often the case that the result you get will show a positive NPV (and therefore qualify you for a federal HAMP modification) while your mortgage servicing company will derive a negative result (which will disqualify you for a HAMP modification). The reason the final outcome

Stop Foreclosure

differs is because the inputs you used were different than the inputs your mortgage servicer used.

Under HAMP guidelines, the program that determines whether you qualify for a HAMP is the same program that is available to you on line. The mortgage servicer may contend that the results differ because they are using a proprietary program (one that is only available to managers with the company that services your mortgage). This is an empty contention. Don't buy into it. Most of the proprietary programs are based on the very same principals.

The Net Present Value (NPV) analysis takes into account all future streams of projected income and expenses that are relevant to your mortgage. Future streams of income received by the mortgage servicers that are paid by you, the homeowner, are discounted by the program to a present value.

A mortgage payment projected to be received 30 years from now is discounted (or reduced significantly) to the value that same payment

Stop Foreclosure

would be expected to have today (in the present). What is the principle here?

One dollar today ($1) is worth more than a dollar received ten years from today. When considering a monthly mortgage payment of say $1,000, a payment you send off to your mortgage servicer today is worth more in present value terms than a payment of $1,000 that you will be making ten years from today.

The present value principal makes sound intuitive sense, doesn't it? Remember the price of a cup of coffee just 10 years ago? It was much less than the price charged by most coffee shops today. You got more for your money back then.

When the various inputs to the Net Present Value analysis are changed the final result (i.e., whether you pass and qualify or fail and are disqualified) can also change. As a homeowner you can always dispute the result that a mortgage servicing company gets if it is negative which disqualifies you from a HAMP loan. Ask them for the specifics on the values they used as inputs to the analysis.

If your analysis showed a Pass and your mortgage servicer tells you (in writing) that you failed, you

©Robert Rodgers, PhD

Stop Foreclosure

may be informed that your mortgage servicer is using a proprietary Net Present Value program. You got a different result because you used a different program. Again, this is a fancy dodge.

Yes, most of the mortgage servicers do have in house proprietary programs that differ somewhat from the NPV online program available to you as a homeowner. The principles that underpin any in house or propriety program and the federal government's NPV program (accessible to you) are the same. The difference will not be due to the programs that were used. It will be driven by a difference in the input values that were used. The program used to determine whether you qualify for a HAMP modification is the program you can use yourself.

For example, the mortgage servicer may have used an input value for the current market value of your home that is $60,000 more than the value you used. This in itself may be a big enough difference to generate a failed outcome.

Keep in mind that when you call your mortgage servicer to discuss this type of issue you are talking with a phone representative who will have

Stop Foreclosure

no clue as to the input values and probably even no idea what a Net Present Value analysis is anyway. They are not trying to make life difficult for you. They just simply have never had any training on this as an issue. Remember, their job is simply to read information from a computer screen that shows the history of your application.

Be clear and assertive if you want to keep your home. Ask every other day when you make your phone inquiries for specifics on the input values the mortgage servicer used (if you failed the analysis and you have determined you should have passed). Ask to speak with the manager who did the analysis.

Do not expect to succeed and actually talk with a manager. The chances that will happen are near zero. But, simply making the request sends a clear signal you are dead serious about securing a modification for your home.

If you derived a positive NPV result and your mortgage servicer informs you that you failed the NPV test, challenge the result that they got. Tell the phone representative that your calculated the NPV analysis yourself and got a positive finding.

©Robert Rodgers, PhD

Stop Foreclosure

Ask the phone representative to enter a comment in your file (on their computer screen) that states exactly that: Your own analysis shows that you passed the test.

You may never find out the values that they used, but they will be influenced by your assertiveness and determination to keep your home. They will also know that if they used different values they would also derive a positive result!

The good news is that you do not have to understand the mathematics behind NPV calculations to have a pretty good idea whether you will pass or fail. Quite frankly, I doubt few of the managers who work for mortgage servicers understand themselves the mathematics behind Net Present Value (NPV) calculations.

Most managers do not even understand the reason why you should consider the present value of a future income stream. It is not good decision making to simply add up the total of payments that are projected over a 20 or 30 or 40 year period. Why? A payment made today is worth significantly more than a payment of the same

Stop Foreclosure

amount that is made twenty years from now. The purchasing power of money erodes over time.

Unknown to most people, mortgage services do not consider, evaluate or rely on results of a Net Present Value (NPV) analysis to determine whether to offer a modification or not. Conducting a Net Present Value (NPV) analysis is merely a federal legal requirement that mortgage servicers have to satisfy if a home owner has submitted a written application for a modification. A home owner must pass the NPV test to qualify for a HAMP modification.

Most modifications are actually in house modifications, not HAMP modifications. The mortgage servicer simply extends an offer to modify a loan at a lower monthly payment after adjusting the interest rate and/or term of the mortgage. . The NPV analysis rarely plays a role in determining whether you will be offered a modification.

Although incentives are offered to mortgage servicers to offer HAMP modification, I suspect that the incentives are not great enough for servicers to place themselves under the thumb

©Robert Rodgers, PhD

and scrutiny of the federal scrutiny and regulations.

A set of input factors (specified in a later section) are required in the Net Present Value analysis (whether it is in house or a HAMP analysis). When the dust settles there are only a few factor inputs that determine the end result: the amount of projected equity in the home (which is determined by an analysis of the values of homes that are comparable to your home) and the "discount rate."

Is Equity Advantageous or Disadvantageous When It Comes to Getting My Home Loan Modified?

What really cuts the mustard when it comes to whether you pass or fail the Net Present Value test? Have you been paying down the principal owed on your mortgage for many years without ever having to refinance? The good news is that you now have a hefty equity. Hooray! That is what you have been working toward all these years. Right?

There is also bad news unfortunately, especially now that you are having difficulty making your

Stop Foreclosure

mortgage payments. You can count on failing the NPV test because you have a juicy chunk of equity in your home. Your mortgage servicer is going to want to gobble up that equity for themselves.

Think of your servicer as a very hungry dog. Equity in your home is by far the most significant factor. Your hungry dog (in the form of your servicer) realizes once you miss a payment that if they act quickly they can scarf up that juicy equity stake right now.

A large equity will thus likely disqualify you from being approved for a HAMP modification. The chances of getting an in house modification from your mortgage servicer are also slim.

You may be thinking the financial institution that holds your mortgage will honor and respect your long history of making timely payments each and every month until recently. Perhaps you have almost paid off your loan until the unfortunate circumstance you confront now (like loss of employment or health problems) created a financial nightmare for you and your family. You certainly never anticipated when you bought your

©Robert Rodgers, PhD

home that you would be in the situation you face today.

The bottom line is simple: Right now you have not been able to pay your mortgage. Maybe you have only a few years left before the debt is cleared? Surely the NPV calculation will take your excellent long term payment history into consideration?

Yes, the Net Present Value analysis takes take into account the hefty equity you have amassed on your home over the years. The analysis however favors the beneficiary (i.e., the mortgage servicers) not you. A large equity is a huge enticement to the financial institution that owns your mortgage note to seize your home through foreclosure and sell it at a hefty profit or convince you to sell it.

What is the Principal Behind a Net Present Value Analysis?

The Net Present Value (NPV) analysis was formulated from the perspective of the beneficiary (or the financial institution that holds your mortgage note). The analysis evaluates the option to foreclosure versus the option to modify the current loan under more favorable conditions

Stop Foreclosure

from a purely cost/benefit analysis. Only the interests of the owner of the mortgage note are relevant, not the home owner. The NPV analysis does not take into account any extenuating circumstances that affect you as the home owner.

If you are dead serious about qualifying for modification to your mortgage, the best situation is to have an equity which is entered into the Net Present Value analysis that is as tiny as possible or even better, negative. A negative equity simply means that you owe more on your home than it is worth.

Equity is calculated by subtracting the difference between the current market value of your home from the mortgage debt. The debt on the property is fixed and nonnegotiable. It is not adjustable.

The current market value of your home on the other is simply a best guess about its value today. The value that is set is always up for challenge, debate and possible adjustment.

The current market value may be a very different figure than the price you originally paid for your home. In some neighborhoods, the market value

Stop Foreclosure

of homes has skyrocketed. The current market value of your home may have doubled or even tripled. This trend would be to your disadvantage in securing a modification to your mortgage.

Of course in other neighborhoods, the market value of homes may have dropped dramatically such that the current market value of your home is half or even a third of the price you paid when it was purchased. This trend will be to your great advantage in obtaining a modification to your mortgage.

How Do I Determine the Current Market Value of My Home?

Rest assured that when your mortgage servicer performs their own Net Present Value (NPV) analysis on your home to decide whether you are qualified to receive a federal Making Home Affordable (HAMP) Modification, they will be motivated to enter a market value that is likely to be higher than the existing market can realistically bear. Always keep in mind that the values that are entered into the analysis (by your mortgage servicer or you) are entirely speculative and thus can be questioned.

©Robert Rodgers, PhD

Stop Foreclosure

Your mortgage servicer will not use a market value for your home that is pure guesswork. It is usually backed up by an analysis of market values in your neighborhood. Unfortunately the analysis is frequently calculated by a company that has no knowledge of the comparable value of homes in the various neighborhood of your town or city.

It is not uncommon for an analysis of comparable housing values in Phoenix, Arizona for example to be conducted by a firm in New York City that has no knowledge whatsoever of the unique factors and circumstances that drive the housing values in Phoenix.

The three properties selected by your mortgage servicer that are presumed to be comparable to your home may actually be located in neighborhoods known to you and every other homeowner in Phoenix to have values that are significantly higher than the values in your own neighborhood. You are much more of an expert about comparable housing in your community than anyone who is doing a distant analysis in (for example) New York City. You have a responsibility and right to challenge a market value that you know is higher than the market will bear.

©Robert Rodgers, PhD

Stop Foreclosure

It is easy to become confused about the result that you ideally want to have. Most homeowners want to see the market value of homes rise in their neighborhood. This means that when and if they decide to sell their home, they will benefit by making an extra profit from the inflated values of real estate.

Requesting a modification to your mortgage loan at a more affordable payment is an entirely different game. You are not selling your home. Your preference is to keep your home by negotiating a more affordable mortgage payment. You therefore would like to use a market value of your home that is a low as possible but still justified based on values of comparable homes that have recently sold.

It is not usually the case that the mortgage servicer is trying to con you. Often the company doing the analysis of the market value of your home simply has no knowledge of the neighborhoods that should be considered as comparable to your own.

©Robert Rodgers, PhD

Stop Foreclosure

How Do I Dispute a Market Analysis of My Home that Has Disqualified Me from Getting a Modification

If the outcome of your own Net Present Value (NPV) test differs from that of your mortgage servicer (i.e., your own analysis shows you passed while the analysis conducted by your mortgage services shows you failed) be sure to find out from your mortgage servicer the name of the company who conducted the comparable housing analysis.

Why? You need to know which properties they used to determine the market value of your home. Locate each of these properties. Make a determination for yourself if the properties are indeed comparable. Prepare a set of arguments that explain why the properties might have been overvalued.

Perhaps your property is located next to a transistor station or an auto body shop. Point this liability out. The homes selected as comparable such be located in neighborhoods with similar circumstances.

Perhaps your property is in a state of disrepair. Point out in writing to your mortgage servicer all

Stop Foreclosure

aspects of your home that need to be replaced or repaired if it were it to be sold.

- Does the roof need to be replaced? Take pictures. Make a case based on the date of the last roof replacement.

- Does the basement leak? Take pictures. Make a case based on evidence from the last flood.

- Does the plumbing need to be replaced? Talk with a plumber. Get them to make an estimate of the repairs that are needed.

- Is the heating outdated and inefficient? Get a heating contractor to prepare a no cost estimate of the cost of repairing the existing unit or replacing it.

You get the point here. Making this case does not mean that you have to make any of these repairs. It simply supports your case of using a market value that is as low as possible. After all, you currently confront an economic hardship. You have not been in a position to make repairs to your home as you would have preferred. The servicer realizes this!

©Robert Rodgers, PhD

Stop Foreclosure

If the mortgage servicer realizes that the home is in serious disrepair they will be more receptive to offering a modification regardless of the amount of equity. Remember, a foreclosure means that your home will now be sold. Who wants to buy a home that is in serious disrepair? If there is a strong suspicion that it will be more trouble to sell the home than to deal with you, they will likely make the better choice of offering you a modification.

Considerations when Doing Your Own Net Present Value Analysis

In doing your own NPV analysis, use a best estimate of the market value of your home that you have calculate based on your own analysis of comparable homes that have recently sold. If you do not know how much a home has sold for that you would like to include in your analysis, ask a realtor. Most are happy to lend a helping hand for free.

Alternatively, you can always get the county or city's assessment of value for the homes you want to use as comparables. This can be to your advantage, since these values in many

Stop Foreclosure

jurisdictions are less than the actual market value of homes. Your mortgage servicer will likely not know this little fact.

Enter the figure you estimate for the market value of your home into the Net Present Value (NPV) calculation. Again, you will want to use the lowest possible figure for the current market value of your home which can be justified on an analysis of recent sales of three comparable homes in your neighborhood. (I do not mean to belabor this point, but many people mistakenly think they need a value for their home that is as high as possible).

By neighborhood I mean the section of housing where the prices of houses are all comparable to the prices of houses in your neighborhood (if no houses have sold recently in your own neighborhood). There may have been sales in your same street, but often the analysis has to include homes outside your immediate neighborhood because there are no recent sales of comparable homes in your neighborhood. Sales should have been closed and reported within the past six months.

©Robert Rodgers, PhD

Stop Foreclosure

Keep in mind that no one knows what the current market value of your home actually is now. You would only know that figure if you sold the house today. The current market value is a best guess that is justified on an analysis that may look scientific. Any market analysis of housing values is very subjective and, to a large extent, entirely arbitrary. A market analysis done be two independent companies could well project two market values that diverge significantly. This is why a mortgage servicer will often average the values of two estimates from two different sources if two are available.

What is a Discount Rate?

The discount rate is an arbitrary rate (entered as a percent) that is entered by your mortgage servicing company which reflects the "risk" that they undertake were they to offer you a loan modification at a lower rate.

In one mediation I attended the mortgage servicer entered a risk of 80% which assured that the home owner would fail the NPV test. The home owner had entered a rate of 3.5% and thus passed the NPV test.

©Robert Rodgers, PhD

Stop Foreclosure

Why did the mortgage servicer use a discount rate of 80% when they did the Net Present Value (NPV) analysis? Because, they said, they did not believe the home owner would make payments on a modified mortgage even if the payment was substantially reduced. The housing counselor who represented the home owner at the mediation vigorously disputed the use of such an outrageously high rate.

You can always dispute any discount rate that your mortgage servicer enters into the NPV analysis. Mortgage servicers have their own proprietary programs, but they are based on the same principles as the program you have access to use when calculating the NPV. The discount rate generally used in a HAMP analysis is set at a reasonably low rate of between 2-3% .

How Can I Calculate the Net Present Value (NPV)

CheckMyNPV.com is a free tool provided by the United States Department of the Treasury, and the Department of Housing and Urban Development in conjunction with the federal Making Home Affordable Program.

©Robert Rodgers, PhD

Stop Foreclosure

CheckMyNPV.com is designed to assist homeowners in conducting a net present value (NPV) evaluation of their mortgage for the Home Affordable Modification Program (HAMP). CheckMyNPV.com can be used by homeowners who have been denied a HAMP modification because of their NPV result.

Homeowners can enter the NPV input values listed in the HAMP Non-Approval Notice received from their mortgage servicer, or substitute with estimated NPV input values, to compare the outcome provided by CheckMyNPV.com against that on the Non-Approval Notice.

This tool can also be used by homeowners prior to applying for a HAMP modification to help them better understand the NPV evaluation. CheckMyNPV.com provides only an estimate of a mortgage servicer's NPV evaluation. While the NPV formula used on CheckMyNPV.com is required to be the same as that of your mortgage servicer's, differences in input data and other industry-related data often result in different outputs.

©Robert Rodgers, PhD

Stop Foreclosure

After getting the Net Present Value result using CheckMyNPV.com, I strongly recommend that you save and print a copy of the evaluation and share it with your mortgage servicer to discuss options available to you.

While free to access and use the Net Present Value Analysis through checkMyNPV.com is a nightmare to use. Many people give up because they did not know that you cannot save your progress as you enter the information required to generate an outcome. If any information is missing the program will not calculate a result.

To avoid pulling all of your hair out and screaming at your friends that the world is unfair, gather together all of the information you will need before you begin entering the information into the NPV program. Why?

The program used to input the data is not - I repeat not - user friendly. Here is why:

- You cannot pause the system.
- You will be disconnected after 15 minutes of inactivity and lose all data that you have entered.

©Robert Rodgers, PhD

Stop Foreclosure

- You can't save your data and come back later to finish. The system does not save any information that you might have already entered.

- You must complete all of the information required on a page before advancing to the next page.

- If you click the back button on your computer at any time while entering the information all of the information will be lost.

- Once you click submit to calculate, your results will be returned in about 10 seconds. If you click submit more than once you will likely have to start all over again because all of your information will be lost.

If you have all the information at your fingertips, you should be able to input all the information required in about 20 minutes from start to finish. Enter inputs to all questions at one sitting. If there is one question on a page left unanswered, the system will freeze up until you provide an answer. If you can't answer a question and there

©Robert Rodgers, PhD

Stop Foreclosure

is inactivity for 15 minutes you will have to start over. Of course, if your computer goes down while you are entering the information, everything you have entered will also be lost and you will have to start over as well.

Spend some time gathering together all the information you will need to complete the Net Present Value Analysis (NPV) before you log on to www.checkmynpv.com and begin entering the information and data. You can always get the free assistance of a housing counselor to assist you in entering the information and generating a result.

Here is a listing of the information you will need to have at your fingertips before you log on and enter the information into the Net Present Value Online Program:

1. Does Fannie Mae or Freddie Mac own your loan?

2. Name of your mortgage servicer

3. Information about your first or "primary" mortgage

4. Current market value of your home

Stop Foreclosure

5. Total monthly income from all sources. If you jointly own the property with another person or spouse, add their income to the total. Details on deriving your total monthly income and understanding what you can and cannot include can be found at:

   https://www.checkmynpv.com/sites/all/themes/npvtool/pdf/CheckMyNPV-Monthly-Gross-Income.pdf

6. A current credit score for both the borrower and if applicable, co-borrower

How Can I Find Out My Credit Score for Free?

The Fair Credit Reporting Act (FCRA) provides you the right to obtain a free copy of your credit report once every 12 months. The FCRA also allows you to obtain your credit score from the three national credit reporting companies for a fee.

To receive a free copy of your credit report, and purchase your credit score, visit

©Robert Rodgers, PhD

Stop Foreclosure

www.AnnualCreditReport.com or call toll-free: 877-322-8228.

I strongly suggest that you complete the worksheet and print it out before you begin inputting the information. Answer all the questions that are found on the worksheet that you will see on the following web page:

https://www.checkmynpv.com/sites/all/themes/npvtool/pdf/CheckMyNPV-Input-Worksheet.pdf

There is a print capability on the website located in the top right corner of the web page above. Hover over the icons and you will locate the icon that says print. Click it and you will be able to save all of your answers.

After Entering All My Information into a Net Present Value Analysis - I Failed. What Can I Do Now?

Big deal I say. Who ever said you could only do one analysis? Start inputting different values to see what numbers will generate a passing score. Pay particular attention to the value you state for the market value of your and the amount of income you declare.

©Robert Rodgers, PhD

Stop Foreclosure

Play around with the numbers. It may be a few more hundred dollars in income or a few thousand dollars less in market value will flip the result from a fail to a pass. You may be closer than you realize. You can exercise the program as many times as you want. It is free to access but a nightmare to use if you are a novice.

Think about it. If you need only a few hundred more dollars in income, it should be possible to generate that much more income through a second job or other part time work. I suggest that you step out of the back seat of the process and plant yourself firmly in the driver's seat. Know what it takes to pass the Net Present Value (NPV) test before you even apply for a modification. Do not let the mortgage servicer convince you that you have failed the NPV analysis when you can show that you can pass it.

Will it Really Help Me Obtain a Modification to My Home Mortgage If Go to All the Trouble of Doing My Own Net Present Value Analysis?

I admit it. It will be a pain to gather all the information you will need to input into the Net

Stop Foreclosure

Present Value (NPV) analysis program which is a big pain to use. And, as noted, it will be helpful to solicit the free assistance of a housing counselor which takes time and effort to set up. Is it really worth all the trouble? Ask yourself:

> **Do I really want to stay in my house?**
>
> **How much effort am I willing to expend to get a modification?**

It is certainly true that mortgage servicers do not even consider Net Present Value (NPV) analyses in deciding whether to offer a modification. It certainly plays no role in decisions to offer in house modifications. Quite frankly, it really does not matter what the final result is unless you are going to be qualified for a HAMP modification (which requires a positive outcome).

What does matter is the mortgage servicer's assessment of your intention, ability and commitment to make payments (under a modified program) reliably and consistently. Keep in mind that as many as half of home owners who are offered modifications default. (This figure goes up and down depending on the current state of the

Stop Foreclosure

economy).

Permit me to put it this way: How many homeowners will bother to actually do their own Net Present Value (NPV) Analysis? I assure you that this number is very small indeed. If you come in with your own result and your own figures, you are making a strong statement to the servicer that you are dead serious about keeping your home no matter what it takes.

Some people who have applied for a modification to their home mortgage actually have no intention of keeping their home. They are simply stalling so that they can stay in their home rent free for as long as possible. In such cases, the home owner and the servicer both benefit from deferring the final decision to foreclose or modify the loan.

- *The home owner gets to stay in their home rent free (sometimes for two years or longer).*

- *The servicer gets to collect all the penalties and fees which have to be paid up front when the property is sold at foreclosure.*

©Robert Rodgers, PhD

Stop Foreclosure

Make it crystal clear to the servicer that you want a modification as soon as possible. The longer a decision is deferred the penalties for nonpayment will mount up quickly. Cut these costs which will have to be paid eventually by demanding an expeditious decision.

I Know Precisely the Mortgage Payment I Can Handle for the Next Several Years. Once I Dig Myself Out of the Mess I am In Right Now, I will be Able to Pay the Original Amount. Should I Ask My Mortgage Servicer to Consider a Two Year (or Short Term) Modification? I Know Now I Will Only Need to Pay the Reduced Amount for a Couple of Years.

My advice would be to forget it. Do not even bother. You do not tell the servicers how to modify your loan. They will tell you what they are willing to offer. Period. End of story. You can make a proposal if you want, but the managers will probably never see it or consider it.

There is another consideration. Servicers are able to modify loans permanently (after the 3 month trial). Quite frankly, they do not have the

Stop Foreclosure

technology to offer custom designed deals to home owners. Even the Making Home Affordable Program is very specific about what deal will be offered.

I suggest that you ...

1. Be completely clear about your intention to keep your home (if that is your intention). Forgive me for repeating this suggestion over and over, but it is important!

2. Give the servicer all the information they need to make a determination.

3. Call them every other day to get the status of your application.

4. Cross your fingers every day for a good outcome.

5. Ask the universe every day to make the best modification possible for you and your family.

Remember, financial institutions do not want to seize your property. They want the stream of income. Their business is money. They are not in the real estate business. It costs a pretty penny to

Stop Foreclosure

foreclose on a property. They would prefer to make money from you at a lower rate than taking the risk of selling the property at a significant loss.

How Will I Hear About the Outcome of My Application?

Be prepared to receive form letters in your snail mailbox at your home that have long lists of possible outcomes. The outcomes that apply to your application will be checked. The form will not be signed by a person but by the "Loan Mitigation Department." It is about as impersonal as a decision letter can get.

The following form letter is an example of a rejection letter that you as a home owner will be likely to receive. If the option applies to you, the circle to the left of the item will be checked.

Rejection Letter

In connection with your request for a modification to your existing mortgage loan we regret to inform you that your request has been denied for the following reason(s):

○ The financial information provided shows you have insufficient income to support approval of

Stop Foreclosure

your application for a modification. We strongly recommend that you consider selling your property. If the market value of your home has declined significantly and would likely not result in a full pay off of your loan if sold, contact our office if and when an offer is received. We will review the offer for a possible short sale.

- The financial information provided shows that your income is sufficient to address your existing mortgage obligation. We are unable to modify your existing obligation.

- While you do not have sufficient income to support all of your monthly expenses, some of your expenses could be reduced. It is recommended that you contact your other creditors with the intent of lowering any and all other monthly obligations. Once you have completed these adjustments, we will conduct a workout review of your case to identify possible solutions.

- Our records indicate that we requested additional information from you which has not been received. Therefore, we are not able to continue a review of your application.

©Robert Rodgers, PhD

Stop Foreclosure

- Our company services your mortgage on behalf of a group of investors that has not given us authority to modify the existing terms of your mortgage.

- The payment we received pursuant to the temporary modification agreement with you does not represent the correct amount as specific in the agreement.

- The payment required under the temporary modification agreement was not received by the due date as specified in the modification agreement.

- We have not received the properly signed and executed documents.

- We have not received the required contribution by the due date.

- We have been unable to resolve outstanding title issues in order to meet recording requirements for your mortgage note.

- Your application for a HAMP is denied due to sufficient cash reserves.

©Robert Rodgers, PhD

Stop Foreclosure

- Your application is under review for another workout

Mortgage servicers are required to evaluate your application initially for a Making Home Affordable Modification. After all the required paperwork has been submitted (which as you now know takes months and months), and a review has been done, many people are rejected for a HAMP.

The rejection letter that I initially received checked the last two entries on the options listed above. First, the entry was checked that we were denied for a HAMP modification due to insufficient reserves. We had not yet spent down our savings. Second, the last entry was checked that the account was in review for another workout.

As you can readily see, the notification process is informal, detached and impersonal. You do not have any clear access to dispute or question any decision that is reached. The rejection letters do not list a contact person to discuss the reason for the rejection. The reason may well be unclear and, in some cases, entirely unjustified.

©Robert Rodgers, PhD

Stop Foreclosure

What should be your response? Remember that your only access to the servicer is through calling the toll free number which puts you in contact with the phone representatives (or clerks). You will never get a manager's email address or their phone number. You will never talk with a person who actually reviewed your application.

Your one and only recourse is to call the servicer's toll free number and dispute the decision. You will likely not get clear answers or any answers, but this should not stop you from making your case. Request that your comments and questions be included in your file. Explain you will be calling back every day for clarification.

OK – so your application has been denied. You have several choices here. You can walk away from engagement with your mortgage servicer, pack up your belongings and move out of your house. You can put your house up for sale. You can stay in your house until the sheriff kicks you out because it is being sold in a foreclosure.

Or, you can dispute the decision. Taking the later action sends a powerful message to the mortgage servicer that you are not walking away from your

Stop Foreclosure

financial obligations and are dead serious about getting your mortgage modified.

I suspect that some servicers routinely reject everyone for some arbitrary reason to just see what they will do in response. Some servicers throw in your face as many obstacles as possible just to see what you will do. Keep in mind that even if a modification is offered, many home owners fail to make their mortgage payments. The servicer wants to know if you are motivated to stay in your home!

When rejected (note here I do not say "if") I recommend that you take immediate action. Let the servicer know you are serious. Refuse to let your application for a modification die on the vine. Keep it alive. If your mortgage servicer insists on initiating a new application for a modification, do it! Expect the best outcome for you and your family no matter how many hurdles you have to fly over.

Will My Mortgage Servicer Give me a Reason for a Denial?

©Robert Rodgers, PhD

Stop Foreclosure

The form letter you receive with a decision gives only vague reasons as you can readily see above. Keep calling the servicer. Ask for the reason why your application was denied. Just because it was denied this week does not mean that it will be denied next week. Persistence pays off.

You must of course justify a certain stream of income to succeed. Loans will not be modified for persons without an income or with an income that could never justify even a reduced payment.

How Can I Dispute Penalties or Late Fees Charged by My Mortgage Servicer?

Under federal law, your mortgage servicer must respond promptly to written inquiries, known as "qualified written requests." If you believe you have been charged a penalty, late fee or some other fee by mistake, or if you have other problems with the servicing of your loan, write to your servicer. Include your account number and explain why you believe your account is incorrect. Send your correspondence to the address the servicer specifies for all written requests. Register your request and sent it priority mail with tracking.

©Robert Rodgers, PhD

Stop Foreclosure

The servicer must send you a written acknowledgment within 20 business days of receiving your inquiry. You know when they received it because you tracked the correspondence. Then, within 60 business days, the servicer must correct your account or determine that it is accurate. The servicer must send you a written notice of the action it took and why, as well as the name and phone number of someone to contact.

Do not subtract any disputed amount from your mortgage payment. Your servicer might consider this a partial payment and refuse to accept it. Your payment might be returned to you or put in a "suspense" or "hold" account until you provide the rest of the payment. Either way, your servicer may charge you a late fee or claim that your mortgage is in default and start foreclosure proceedings.

My Mortgage Servicer Says that Extending the Term of My Loan from 30 to 40 Years is Not an Option. Are They Bluffing?

Yes, you will hear this reason often and it may very well be accurate. This may or may not be

Stop Foreclosure

true. Demand to see a copy of the servicing agreement. You should make this request in writing (through registered mail).

If there is an explicit restriction on extending the term of the loan in the servicing agreement, ask your mortgage servicer to request a modification of the servicing agreement. They will try and claim that the servicing agreement cannot be modified. Any servicing agreement can be modified. Many agreements are modified all the time. If the servicer claims it cannot be modified, let them know that it can be modified if a request is made to do so. (Be a little lenient on them. The manager may actually not realize that any servicing agreement can be modified.)

If the loan is an FHA loan, a request for a modification to the servicing agreement (if it bars a modification in the terms of a loan, especially the term) is legally required when a modification has been requested by the home owner.

Restrictions on extending the term of a loan are often written into many servicing agreements because the lien holder often does not get paid until the end of the existing term of the loan. If

Stop Foreclosure

the term is extended, the wait period before they are paid is also extended.

Just because the current servicing agreement precludes an extension does not mean that this constraint cannot be modified. The holder of your mortgage note might readily recognize the benefit of allowing a modification to your loan.

In summary ...

1. If the mortgage servicer tells you that the loan cannot be extended ask them why.

2. If they tell you that the servicing agreement precludes a loan modification demand to see a copy of the servicing agreement.

3. If you confirm that the servicing agreement does in fact preclude a modification, ask the mortgage servicer to request a modification to the servicing agreement.

Modifications are not all that uncommon. Holders of the note more often than not agree to modify the existing service agreement.

©Robert Rodgers, PhD

Stop Foreclosure

What Are My Options If My Income Does Not Justify a Modified Loan?

You have totaled your income from all sources. You have taken 31% of this total income which represents that mortgage that you qualify for. This amount however is not large enough to justify even a modified loan on your home even if the mortgage servicing company agrees to reduce your interest rate to 1% and extend the term of your loan out to 40 years. Is the deal off? Is there no chance of success here?

Perhaps not. If you do not have sufficient income, you will not succeed in securing a modified loan. The key issue always turns on how much equity you have in your home. If you have a lot of equity, the game is over. You will be foreclosed. If you have no equity or negative equity (if you owe more than the home is worth on the market today) the game is not over. It may well be a better decision to give you a chance to pay a loan at a low interest rate that has been extended before initiating foreclosure proceedings. In house modifications in such circumstances are not that uncommon when the mortgage servicing

Stop Foreclosure

company is convinced that you will be able to make the lower payments in a timely fashion.

I am Currently Unemployed. Is There any Hope for Me? What Programs Exist for People Who Want to Remain in Their Homes?

Are you a homeowner facing a financial hardship due to unemployment? If your mortgage is owned by Freddie Mac (and many are) you may be eligible for temporary relief through unemployment forbearance options offered by your mortgage servicer (the organization to which you send your mortgage payments). These options allow for a reduction or suspension of your mortgage payments for a period of up to 12 months. The intention of this program is to help you with your mortgage challenges while you are unemployed.

You may be eligible if:

1. You have a financial hardship due to unemployment.

2. You occupy the property as your primary residence.

©Robert Rodgers, PhD

Stop Foreclosure

3. *Your mortgage is owned by Freddie Mac.*

The Unemployment Forbearance program offers two Options

Short-Term Forbearance Option

If you qualify, your servicer can offer you short-term forbearance for six months, where your mortgage payments are either suspended or reduced. For this option, you:

- May be either current or delinquent in your mortgage payments.

- May convert to this short-term forbearance plan if you lose your job while participating in either a Home Affordable Modification program (HAMP) or Freddie Mac Standard Modification trial period plan.

Extended Unemployment Forbearance Option

If you remain unemployed when the short-term forbearance period ends, your servicer will evaluate your eligibility for extended unemployment forbearance and may extend your forbearance period for up to another six months if

Stop Foreclosure

you are eligible. Under this option, your mortgage payments may be reduced or suspended.

How Do I Find Out If Freddie Mac Owns My Loan?

Find out if Freddie Mac owns your loan. If they do, you may want to pursue the unemployment forbearance option which will provide a welcome cushion while you search for another job.

https://ww3.freddiemac.com/corporate/

I was offered a Temporary Modification but was only One (1) Day Late Making the Second Payment. We were Serviced a Foreclosure Notice Today. Can the Bank Foreclosure Now When They have Already Agreed to a Modification?

Yes, they can and they will. The condition that you make payments on the temporary modification on time is a condition of getting a permanent modification. If you have succeeded in securing a temporary modification you must make each of the tree payments on time. If you are even a day

Stop Foreclosure

late, the deal is off. You might as well start shopping around for a new place to live.

The Bank Has Offered a Modification but the Rate is Still Too Much for My Pocketbook. They Say that They Cannot Offer me a HAMP (the federal program which would make the payment more affordable) because I Have Been Delinquent in Making Payments for More than One Year. Should I just Give Up Now?

Talk about total frustration here. This happens frequently. Why is the loan now more than a year delinquent? Because the mortgage servicing company keeps asking for more and more documentation and delaying the process using one excuse after another. (This is why it is so important that you stay on their case every other day).

They are correct in that your application for a modification does not qualify for a HAMP. Can you possibly begin making payments? If so, you are no longer delinquent for longer than a year. At some point (and it would depend on the details of the law which are changing all the time) you might be

Stop Foreclosure

in a position to qualify for a HAMP loan at a low rate.

You can always re-apply for a loan modification. There is no law that precludes this option. Remember, most modifications are in-house anyway.

What is a Three Month Temporary Loan Modification? I Asked for a Permanent Modification to my Mortgage Loan.

Every permanent modification to a home loan is preceded by a three month temporary modification plan. Once a new payment amount has been set (which can in some cases involve a forbearance of some of the principal, an extension of the term of the loan, a reduction in the interest rate or all of the above) you must make each of the three payments on time each of the three months. The lender wants to see evidence that you are in a position to make the payments under the modified agreement before the modification is converted to a permanent loan status. If you are a day late, the deal is off.

The system that has been used to issue temporary modifications continues to change. Initially, there

Stop Foreclosure

was a brief agreement for a temporary modification which took the form of a one page letter which specified the arrangement to pay a reduced amount for three months. The permanent modification agreement is prepared and forwarded only after all three payments have been made on time. Servicers did not want to prepare the permanent modification paperwork before seeing that a home owner could meet the monthly obligation under the terms of the modified agreement.

More recently, a single permanent modification document is prepared and forwarded to the homeowner for signature that includes provisions that the first three payments must be made on time for the permanent modification to take effect.

Is the Deal Done When I Get a Written Offer of a Modification?

Take nothing for granted when it comes to securing a modification to your home mortgage. There are cases where homeowners succeed in getting a temporary loan modification. They make all of their payments on time according to the

Stop Foreclosure

terms of the temporary modification agreement. After three months, the servicer claims there is a deficiency of payment. They return the checks to the home owner and foreclose.

Send your temporary modification payments by registered, priority mail at least one week before the payment is due. Require a receipt and signature from the mortgage servicer on each mailing.

Read the temporary modification agreement or letter carefully. Pay particular attention to where you are instructed to make the initial three payments. Do not arbitrarily send the payment to the address you are accustomed to sending your regular mortgage payments. Payments required under temporary loan modifications often must be sent to a different address. Use the address given in the correspondence that describes conditions for the temporary modification. Read the letter 6 times (or more) to make sure you have not missed anything that you are required to do.

Check your bank statements to verify that the bank has deposited your payment. If it was not

Stop Foreclosure

deposited, immediately initiate an inquiry to determine why the payment was not deposited. Your bank can also place a hold on the check and wire payment to the servicer the same day.

I was told by a Clerk about the Terms of a Temporary Modification but Cannot Tell if this is a Genuine Offer. The Offer Seemed Very Unprofessional to Me.

I mediated a case where the mortgage servicing company refused to offer the home owner a modification because they had already turned down an offer for a modification. Why? The home owner said that they were not convinced it was an authentic offer so they simply ignored it. This was a big mistake on the home owner's part.

If you have any such doubts about the authenticity of an offer, call the mortgage servicing company immediately and ask for a confirmation that the modification offer is authentic. You will only get one chance here for a modification. This is not a baseball game where you get three strikes and you are out. One strike and the game is over.

©Robert Rodgers, PhD

Stop Foreclosure

What Can I Realistically Expect If a Modification is Offered? How Much Lower Can I Expect My Payment to Be?

I certainly do not want to dash your hopes for the deal of a lifetime – and certainly any outcome is possible when it comes to modifying home loans. Realistically speaking – and I have now seen the terms of quite a few modifications – you will be lucky to see a reduction in your monthly payment of 20 to 25%. In some cases, the modification is only slightly less than the original payment you had agreed to make when you purchased the home. One reason is that the payments you have failed to make are sometimes added to the principal which is used to calculate the payment you must now make under the modified arrangement.

Several years ago I asked a representative from Wells Fargo what the most common offer looked like. The answer was that the most common offer was to extend the term of the loan out to 40 years. In some cases, the interest rate was lowered by no more than 1% or 2%.

©Robert Rodgers, PhD

Stop Foreclosure

Yes, you will read discussions of possibilities that the principal amount will be forgiven or set aside. If forgiven it is written off. I have never seen such an offer myself but have heard of one case where that happened. Alternatively, a specific part of the principal can be set aside with no interest applied, though the principal that was set aside must still be paid when the remainder of the loan has been paid. These deals sound great, eh? Don't get your hopes up. They are rare.

Might I point out however that a modification offer (even if not that advantageous given your original agreement) may not be all that disadvantageous? You were probably able to stop making payments for a number of months. In some cases the term of a free ride can be as long as two years. You may have had the benefit of not having to make payments for an extended period of time.

Some modifications set aside all of the payments that were not made along with the penalties that were assessed, with no interest applied. Obviously, this can be a great benefit. Any

Stop Foreclosure

amounts that have been "set aside" are typically due as a balloon payment at that point in time when the principal has been paid off. If you cannot make this payment – the servicer will have a strong incentive to foreclose as expeditiously as possible. This may not look like such a great deal years from now when the principal has been paid off and the balloon payment is due.

Do not set your expectations too low however! The mortgage business is a moving target. Every week brings changes. You never know what to expect. Set high expectations and let your servicer know every other day when you call in that you are serious about keeping your home. Your intent and honesty and integrity counts for something when it comes to getting your home mortgage modified.

Aren't the Mortgage Companies the Bad Guys Here?

You have certainly read and probably heard many stories of slimy actions by mortgage companies. As with any organizations, there are good ones and bad ones. There are ones with integrity and those without. So yes, some mortgage companies

Stop Foreclosure

are the bad guys, but not all of them are scum bags.

And guess what? Some home owners are the bad guys in the equation. Some home owners are being deceitful. Some lie. Some cannot be trusted to take their grandmother to the grocery store without stealing the money in her purse.

Mortgage companies have to deal with the full range of home owners – those who have integrity and those who do not. They do not know which of the two you are. Make it your business to demonstrate that:

1. *You do have integrity.*
2. *You have been truthful in everything you have submitted in your application.*
3. *You will pay your temporary mortgage on time.*
4. *You will pay your future mortgage payments as agreed.*

Stop Foreclosure

What if I also have a Second Mortgage or Line of Credit on the Property?

Until recently the only active player in the loan modification game was the company that serviced the first or primary mortgage. This has recently changed. Now, the companies that service second mortgages and lines of credit (LOC) are becoming much more aggressive in demanding payment and even issuing foreclosure notices. You may need to negotiate with more than one mortgage servicing company if you wish to succeed in securing a modification to your loan which is affordable.

How Do I Find a Housing Counselor?

You will likely receive notices (or come across offers) from many companies and individuals claiming they can save your house and/or guarantee you a HAMP modification. Such offers are often tied to a heavy price tag in the thousands of dollars. My advice is to not take the bait. Sure it would be great if someone else could do this for you even if it cost several thousand dollars. But they cannot do it for you. You need to be involved in the application process personally.

©Robert Rodgers, PhD

Stop Foreclosure

The best resources do not cost any money. One such resource is access to a housing counselor that costs you nothing. Your mortgage servicing company will provide you with notification that you have the right to receive free counseling from a housing counselor. Housing counselors can provide invaluable support and assistance, especially when they have a good handle on current law. There is nothing to lose by seeking free counseling.

Like any profession, the quality of expertise flops all over the place. Some counselors are amazing: they are up to date on the current laws and offer advice that is golden. Other counselors are novices: they have been hired recently and have very little training.

While every state has housing counselors, they can be very short staffed. Your opportunity to receive in depth assistance may be severely limited because the counselors cannot begin to meet the demands for their services.

If you are attempting to apply for a modification to your home loan - or if you have simply missed making one or more payments – consulting with a

Stop Foreclosure

housing counselor can be beneficial before making a decision on how to proceed.

The following website contains a listing of all housing counselors across the United States. This is a free service that is supported by the federal government. Visit the website below. Click on your state. A complete list of counselors and their contact information will be shown.

http://www.hud.gov/offices/hsg/sfh/hcc/fc/

Alternatively, you can talk with a real person to obtain support and information. Call 1-888-995-HOPE for free personalized advice from housing counseling agencies certified by the U.S. Department of Housing and Urban Development (HUD). This national hotline – open 24/7 – is operated by the Homeownership Preservation Foundation, a nonprofit member of the HOPE NOW Alliance of mortgage industry members and HUD-certified counseling agencies. For free guidance online, visit www.hopenow.com.

©Robert Rodgers, PhD

Stop Foreclosure

Are the Laws Governing Modifications to Mortgages Really That Complicated?

As a mediator, I have observed many disputes across the table about what the current law says. The lawyer for the mortgage servicing company argues that they cannot set aside or forgive any of the principal balance (which will lower the mortgage payment). The lawyer for the home owner argues there is nothing in the current regulations that precludes this possibility.

It is sometimes a matter of interpretation. The language in mortgage laws is vague and obtuse. It was written in a confusing way so lawyers could argue over what it all means and eat up our savings.

The most perplexing challenge is that the laws are always changing. What was lawful today may be unlawful tomorrow and vice versa. I would simply say that if you are told that the mortgage servicing company cannot do something, demand to see evidence of this claim as it is specified in the existing laws or servicing agreements. As noted, if there is an explicit prohibition in the servicing agreement ask the mortgage servicing company

©Robert Rodgers, PhD

Stop Foreclosure

(the company you pay your mortgage to) to ask the holders of the lien to modify the agreement.

My Mortgage Servicing Company Refuses to Offer a Modification to My Loan that I am Fully Qualified to Receive (by My Own Calculation) Under the Net Present Value Test. What Can I Do?

You can contact the trustee if you live in a state that is governed by non-judicial procedures for foreclosures. Why hasn't the trustee protected your interests already?

It is not their job. If the borrower brings up a concern to them directly, they will listen. You can tell the trustee:

> *"I have a solution that my servicer refuses to acknowledge."*

The trustee will likely know nothing about this solution unless you tell them. It is not the trustee's duty to investigate information the servicing company has given them. Most trustees do what the servicer's tell them unless they hear from the borrower. Speak up if you then your

©Robert Rodgers, PhD

Stop Foreclosure

rights have been violated or if an option is being discarded that will solve your current problem.

Foreclosure Process

Foreclosure processes are different in every state. If you are worried about making your mortgage payments, you need to learn about the laws in your state that govern the foreclosure process.

The process differs considerably depending on where you live. In some states the notices must be mailed. In others they must be posted on the property. Redemption periods vary considerably. Procedures regulating lawful notices that must precede a foreclosure auction also vary widely. A general overview of what to expect can be found on the Housing and Urban Development's foreclosure timeline.

In general, mortgage companies start foreclosure processes about 3-6 months after the first missed mortgage payment. Late fees are typically charged 15 days after a payment is due. Most mortgage servicing companies recognize that homeowners

Stop Foreclosure

may be facing short-term financial hardships which may well resolve in a month or two. It is always important that you stay in continuous contact with your lender after missing a payment.

After 30 days, the borrower is technically in default and the foreclosure processes is officially accelerated. If you do not call the servicer and ignore the calls demanding payment the foreclosure process will begin much earlier. At any time during the process, it is always a wise decision to discuss with your housing counselor the various options that can be considered to resolve the problem.

Judicial Versus Non-Judicial Foreclosures

Some states – particularly those located in the eastern US - have laws that require judicial foreclosures. In such states, the beneficiary must seek a court order requiring foreclosure on a property. States with judicial foreclosure laws require courts to be involved. Such procedures are time consuming and expensive partly because lawyers have their fingers into the pot.

©Robert Rodgers, PhD

Stop Foreclosure

Mortgages in states with judicial foreclosure laws involve mortgage documents that are executed between two parties – the lender and the borrower. No trustee is involved.

Other states have non-judicial foreclosure procedures which is the case in my state of Washington. Here, the mortgage agreements involve three parties – the lender, the borrower and the trustee (who is typically listed as MERS). The trustee can foreclosure without a court order as long as all of the legal requirements have been satisfied (such as the specification of waiting periods and notices that must be issued to the home owner).

Laws that govern the foreclosure in the various states are continuously changing these days. It will be very helpful if you are fully briefed and up to date on the current laws which government foreclosures in the state where you home is located.

For a preview of the current laws governing foreclosures in your state visit,

http://www.foreclosurelaw.org/

©Robert Rodgers, PhD

Stop Foreclosure

Foreclosures

Three types of foreclosures may be initiated depending on the applicable state law: judicial, power of sale and strict foreclosure. All types of foreclosure require public notices to be issued and all parties to be notified regarding the proceedings. Once properties are sold through an auction, families have a short period of time to find a new place to live and move out before the sheriff issues an eviction.

Judicial Foreclosure
All states allow this type of foreclosure. Some require it. The lender files suit with the judicial system. The borrower then receives note in the mail demanding payment. The borrower then has 30 days to respond with a payment in order to avoid foreclosure. If payment is not made by the deadline specified in the notice, the property is sold through an auction to the highest bidder, carried out by a local court or the local sheriff's office.

©Robert Rodgers, PhD

Stop Foreclosure

Power of Sale

This type of foreclosure, also known as statutory foreclosure, is allowed by many states if the mortgage documents include a *power of sale* clause. After a homeowner has defaulted on mortgage payments, the lender sends out notices demanding payment. Once an established waiting period has passed, the mortgage company, rather than local courts or sheriff's office, carries out a public auction. Non-judicial foreclosure auctions are often more expedient, though they may be subject to judicial review to ensure their legality.

Strict Foreclosure

A small number of states allow this type of foreclosure. In strict foreclosure proceedings, the lender files a lawsuit on the homeowner that has defaulted. If the borrower cannot pay the mortgage within a specific timeline ordered by the court, the property goes directly back to the mortgage holder. Generally, strict foreclosures take place only when the debt amount is greater than the value of the property.

©Robert Rodgers, PhD

Stop Foreclosure

FHA Loan Modifications

What type of mortgage loan do you have? Is it an FHA or VA mortgage? The restrictions and guidelines differ considerably depending on the type of loan you are attempting to modify. Below are the FHA guidelines (which of course can be modified at any time).

Configuration of an FHA Modification

- *Interest Rate shall be reduced to market rate*
- *Loan Term extended to 360 months*
- *Capitalization of delinquent PITI*
- *Legal fees and related foreclosure costs may be capitalized*
- *Allows a loan to be reinstated and results in a payment the mortgagor can afford*

Requirements for an FHA Modification

- *Three (3) payments due and unpaid (or a total of 61 days delinquent)*
- *Minimum of 12 months elapsed since loan origination date*

Stop Foreclosure

- *If an Adjustable Rate Mortgage, the loan must be converted to fixed interest rate*
- *Loan may not be in foreclosure when modification executed*
- *No appraisal or broker price opinion required*

Conditions for an FHA Modification

- *Home owner has a stable monthly income that is sufficient to support the modified mortgage*
- *Home owner is an owner-occupant, committed to occupying property as primary residence*
- *Home Owner does not have another FHA-insured mortgage*

Other Options to Avoid Foreclosure

Loan modifications permanently change one or more of the original mortgage terms (usually the interest rate and term of the loan) to make the monthly payment more affordable. If current income does not qualify you for a modification even at a substantially lower monthly payment,

Stop Foreclosure

other options can be considered that will avoid foreclosure.

Forbearance Agreement

When you can make a strong case that the interruption in income is due to temporary circumstances (such as loss of a job by a person well qualified to obtain employment elsewhere) a Forbearance Agreement may well be a viable option to pursue. Forbearance agreements temporarily let a borrower pay less than the full amount of his or her mortgage payment or, alternatively, pay nothing at all during the forbearance period.

Monthly payments may be suspended for up to three months or reduced for up to six months. A long term forbearance agreement lasts up to 12 months. The mortgage must be brought current at end of the forbearance period.

Partial Reinstatement and Repayment Plan

Has the reason for the interruption in income resolved? Are you now in a position to make a monthly payment but you still owe a considerable sum in unpaid payments and late fees? Consider

Stop Foreclosure

the option of a partial reinstatement and repayment plan.

This arrangement is a formal agreement between the borrower and the mortgage servicing company that gives the borrower a fixed amount of time to bring delinquent mortgage payments current. This is accomplished by paying the normal monthly payment plus an additional amount over a specified period of time. Although the total payment is higher, you can be brought back into a current payment status gradually over a period of time.

Reinstatement

Have you been having financial difficulties with making your mortgage payments? Are you now seriously delinquent and confront an eminent foreclosure? As from the recent hardship, have you recently been the beneficiary of an unexpected sum of money through an inheritance or other gifting? If so, consider a reinstatement of your loan.

A reinstatement is an agreement to pay a lump sum of the total amount past due by a specific date which will usually include all late fees in

Stop Foreclosure

addition to missed mortgage payments. This will bring your situation up to date but will not change the conditions of the mortgage or reduce the amount of payment that is due each month.

Deed-in-Lieu of Foreclosure

Under this settlement arrangement, the mortgagor voluntarily deeds collateral property in exchange for a release from all debt obligations under the mortgage. Typically the first mortgage must be only lien on property. Alternatively, the junior lien holder must release their lien on the property (which would be very rare indeed). Some Deed-in-Lieu of Foreclosure programs compensate the borrower a lump sum up to $2000.

This option appears to be a simple and straightforward way out of a difficult situation. It may well be an option you might want to pursue (though I would strongly recommend that you discuss this option with a housing counselor first).

From my experience, however, it is rarely invoked. The lenders are really not interested in taking ownership of property. Their interest is focused solely on securing a reliable stream of income.

©Robert Rodgers, PhD

Stop Foreclosure

Lenders are only interested in even considering this option if there is a significant equity in the home. Under such circumstances, a home owner will typically find that selling the house themselves rather than deeding it over to the mortgage company yields a more rewarding resolution financially. Still, a deed in lieu of foreclosure is one of the several options that can be considered and works well for some people.

Short Sale

A short sale is the sale of a property by the homeowner for less than the total amount necessary to satisfy any and all debt on the property (including the first mortgage and all other loans on the property). In such a circumstance, a shortfall results when the total sum of money from a sale of the home is less than the amount that is required to pay off all the debt. Short sales are typically considered when:

1. The borrower has a potential buyer for the property.

2. The sale will net less than the borrower owes on all mortgages and lines of credit.

Stop Foreclosure

3. The borrower can't or doesn't want to keep home.

Some home owners see the writing on the wall. Their income at the present time is simply not sufficient to justify a modification, even if the interest rate is lowered to 0% and the term is extended to 40 years. Unable to meet their monthly mortgage commitments they make the difficult decision to sell their home.

A real estate agent is hired. If you employ a reputable agent who knows the foreclosure law in your state, they will deal directly with the servicer to insure that there is a clear understanding of any future debt obligations you may ne required to accept. Do not sign a sales contract agreeing to sell your property and then present the contract to your servicer. Communicate with your servicer first before even putting the house on the market.

You sign an agreement with your real estate agent. Your home is placed on the market. A sale price is set that appears at the outset to be sufficient to pay off all the debt. If sold at the listing price, you as the homeowner will be clear of any future debts or obligations.

©Robert Rodgers, PhD

Stop Foreclosure

Months pass. Several offers are put on the property, but all offers are well below the listing price. You as the home owner continue to wait patiently for a more favorable offer. Meanwhile, a foreclosure notice has been issued. The clock is ticking away with less and less time to finalize a sale before your home is sold through a foreclosure.

Finally, you as the home owner decide to accept a bid on the home which is $10,000 less than the listing price. This is why the sale is called a **short sale**. The sale price of the home is short of what is required to pay off all of the debt obligations on the property.

At the closing, you as the home owner are surprised to discover that you must sign a note of obligation to the mortgage company for $10,000. In other words, you have dug yourself out of a huge mortgage debt only to learn that you continue to have a smaller debt obligation to satisfy. The long ordeal continues to fester.

The bottom line is this. With most short sales, the home owner will often still incur a future debt if the sale of the house does not result in a full

©Robert Rodgers, PhD

Stop Foreclosure

payoff of all liens and mortgages on the home. If a borrower is between 5-10 months behind in payments, they may well find a foreclosure to be more beneficial to them in the long run than agreeing to a short sale.

With a foreclosure, the home owner loses their home, but does not incur any additional debt. A foreclosure ends the long and tedious ordeal. You as the home owner get to settle into a new home somewhere else and start a new life so to speak.

If the servicer (or the phone representative) tells you over the phone that no additional debt will be incurred with a short sale, ask to get that commitment in writing before you agree to sell your property. What happens in practice can diverge from what is promised in a phone call. Remember – these discussions are never documented in emails so you have no proof that the servicer agreed to release you of all debt obligations when you home is sold in a short sale. See it in writing before you believe it.

I have heard horror stories of how the entire process of a short sale has gone array. In one case, the homeowner found a buyer who agreed to a

©Robert Rodgers, PhD

Stop Foreclosure

short sale. The mortgage servicer was notified and approved the sale. But the servicing company failed to cancel the trustee's sale. The property was foreclosed before the sale could be finalized. Do not assume that the servicer has notified the trustee of a short sale on the property.

The bottom line here is to figure if anything will go wrong, it will. Find out the name and address of the trustee. You have a right to contact the trustee directly. Verify from them that the foreclosure proceedings have been suspended. Do this verification even if the mortgage servicing company claims that the trustee sale has been delayed or cancelled (either through phone communication or in writing). I recommend you request written confirmation from the trustee that the foreclosure proceedings have been canceled.

Foreclosure

Foreclosure may actually be the preferred option if you owe more on the home than it is currently worth in the marketplace. If this happens to be your case, you can elect to simply stop making

Stop Foreclosure

mortgage payments. Stockpile whatever payments you can make into a savings account.

You can always apply for a modification (though you can determine from reading my explanations above that a modification will unlikely be approved). Some states provide for mediation for an option which also delays the foreclosure process. You may be able to pursue a foreclosure mediation which automatically delays a foreclosure. In a state like Washington your request for a foreclosure mediation must be forwarded by a housing counselor or a lawyer. You cannot initiate the request directly as a home owner.

The idea is to remain in your home rent free for as long as possible. You may be able to stay in your home for as long as one to two years, enabling a reserve of funds to accumulate in a savings account which can be used to secure alternative housing arrangements (whether rental property or a new home purchase). Again, the procedures are being streamlines, so this time line is being shortened considerably.

©Robert Rodgers, PhD

Stop Foreclosure

Yes, your credit rating will be trashed because you are not paying your mortgage. And yes, it will be difficult to get a new home loan from a lender because of your lousy credit rating.

There are housing alternatives for people who have horrible credit ratings. A market of homes exists that are sold by owners - For Sale By Owner Homes - who do not necessary apply the strict standards of a lending agency. Some owners will even finance your loan without having to go through the scrutiny of a financial institution.

Some owners who sell their homes on a "For Sale by Owner" basis do not contract with a real estate agent. The seller deals directly with them to negotiate a sales arrangement. One possibility is to rent initially, but have the owner agree to apply the rent toward a previously agreed purchase price for the home. If you look hard and long enough, you may well be able to find housing that meets your current financial situation and those of your family quite nicely even if your credit rating is in the basement.

In summary, no one wants to have their home foreclosed. Foreclosure, however, may actually be

©Robert Rodgers, PhD

Stop Foreclosure

your best option at the present time if you are not earning sufficient income to support a modification to your existing home mortgage.

Bankruptcy

Bankruptcy is really not a long term solution for most people interested in keeping their homes. It is a viable option for far fewer people than who actually pursue it as an option. Why is this so?

In bankruptcy, the debt obligation on the home is not forgiven or released. The question that must be addressed in a bankruptcy is this: Can the homeowner afford a payment plan that allows them to keep the home? The borrower must come up with a plan to pay the mortgage payment.

In the long run, your situation is potentially much improved if you can convince your servicer to modify your mortgage and reduce the payment that is due. Bankruptcy does not do this for you.

Mediation

Some states have enacted laws that require mediation between the home owner and the mortgage servicing company before a foreclosure

Stop Foreclosure

can occur. The states of Nevada, Rhode Island, New Jersey, Florida and Washington have enacted such laws. Evidence from states that required mediation reveals that roughly half or more of all mediated cases are settling with borrowers remaining in their homes.

Mediation is not automatic in most states. The home owner must request mediation. For example, in Washington the request for mediation must actually be forwarded by either a lawyer or a housing counselor. The home owner cannot request mediation directly. There are typically costs associated with a mediation, but they are inconsequential relative to the potential benefits.

An important value of mediation to the home owner is the opportunity to have a direct dialogue with the mortgage servicer manager who has the authority to make the decision on whether you will be offered a modification or not. This is not a face to face dialogue, but a conversation conducted through a phone conversation during the mediation. In Washington state, the dialogue with the decision maker is always conducted over

©Robert Rodgers, PhD

Stop Foreclosure

the phone. I understand that other states with foreclosure mediation laws have a similar process.

The home owner never meets the decision maker face to face. The servicer's lawyer is always physically present during the mediation. Home owners have the right to be represented by a lawyer or a housing counselor during mediation.

It is also incredibly helpful to see all of the documentation used by the servicer to evaluate your case. A mediator collects these documents for you. You would be surprised to discover the number of situations involving errors of fact or omissions in the information used buy servicers to evaluate an application for a modification. The home owner has an opportunity in mediation to see all of the evidence that the servicer is using to make a decision and the opportunity to challenge its accuracy. As a home owner seeking a modification you want to insure that all of the information that the servicer has at hand is correct and accurate in every respect.

I strongly recommend that you take the advantage of mediation if the law in your state supports it. Apply as early as possible since there

©Robert Rodgers, PhD

Stop Foreclosure

is always a point specified in all states with foreclosure mediation laws when he process of foreclosure is too far along to initiate a mediation.

Many people are misled by the use of the term mediation which historically requires that both parties come to the table voluntarily and have agreed to discuss the issues in good faith. Mortgage servicers are always one of the parties to any foreclosure mediation. They do not participate voluntarily. The state law requires that they participate. Such discussions are actually conferences that are facilitated by a third party. In most cases, the third party is a trained mediator.

Useful Resources

It's Time We Talked: Mandatory Mediation in the Foreclosure Process

http://www.americanprogress.org/issues/2009/06/time_we_talked.html

Information About Foreclosure Mediation Programs in the Various States

http://www.nclc.org/foreclosures-and-mortgages/foreclosure-mediation-programs.html

©Robert Rodgers, PhD

Stop Foreclosure

Net Present Value Calculator

http://www.fdic.gov/consumers/loans/prevention/NPVCalculator.html

Learning Center at Freddie Mac

http://www.freddiemac.com/learn/

Federal Making Home Affordable Federal Program HAMP/HARP FAQ's and Policy

http://www.hampadmin.com

Industry Mortgage Rate Weekly Updates

http://www.freddiemac.com/pmms/mobile.html

The Five Top Foreclosure Myths

http://www.YouTube.com/freddiemac

Loss Mitigation Services: How To Avoid Foreclosure

http://portal.hud.gov/hudportal/HUD?src=/program_offices/housing/sfh/nsc/lossmit

Index

"in house" modifications, 49
appraisal, 18, 22, 158
Back-End Ratio, 47
bank statements, 31, 33, 34, 36, 43, 46, 76, 77, 142
Bankruptcy, 169, 170
cash reserves, 15, 127

credit rating, 14, 30, 168, 169
Credit Score, 117
current market value, 18, 96, 103, 104, 110, 111
Debt-to-Income Ratio, 47
deed of trust, 54, 64, 69

©Robert Rodgers, PhD

Stop Foreclosure

Deed-in-Lieu of Foreclosure, 161, 162
default-related services, 88, 89
discount rate, 100, 111, 112
documentation, 30, 31, 32, 34, 35, 36, 37, 41, 73, 85, 139, 171
Documentation, 30, 31, 33, 35
equity, 17, 18, 22, 25, 26, 27, 28, 50, 100, 101, 102, 103, 109, 135, 162
Fair Credit Reporting Act, 117
fair market value, 20, 22
Fannie Mae, 48, 57, 62, 117
FAXING, 29
FHA loan, 133
first mortgage, 17, 18, 161, 163
Forbearance Agreement, 159
Foreclosure, 69, 138, 152, 159, 167, 169, 173, 174
foreclosure mediations, 25, 51
Foreclosure Notice, 69, 138
Foreclosure Process, 152, 173
Foreclosures, 154, 155
Freddie Mac, 48, 62, 117, 136, 137, 138, 173
gross income, 40
HAMP, 13, 24, 25, 78, 90, 91, 92, 93, 94, 96, 99, 100, 101, 104, 112, 113, 121, 127, 128, 137, 139, 148, 173
hardship, 24, 28, 31, 32, 52, 53, 84, 91, 108, 136, 161
Housing Counselor, 148
in house modifications, 99, 120
income, 13, 15, 17, 24, 25, 29, 30, 31, 32, 33, 34, 36, 37, 40, 41, 42, 43, 44, 45, 46, 47, 48, 49, 50, 51, 52, 54, 74, 77, 87, 90, 91, 94, 98, 117, 119, 124, 125, 126, 131, 134, 135, 158, 159, 160, 162, 163, 169
interest rate, 13, 24, 28, 82, 87, 88, 99, 135, 140, 144, 158, 159, 163
IRS Form 4506T-EZ, 34
Judicial Foreclosure, 156
judicial foreclosures, 154
late fees, 29, 38, 44, 45, 58, 79, 82, 87, 160, 161
Lines of Credit, 17
loan modification, 9, 10, 11, 17, 22, 26, 27, 40, 67, 70, 83, 111, 134, 140, 141, 147
Loan Modifications, 157
market value, 19, 20, 21, 26, 104, 105, 106, 107, 108, 109, 110, 111, 117, 119, 125
mediation, 60, 112, 167, 170, 171, 172, 173
Mediation, 170, 173
MERS, 59, 60, 61, 62, 63, 154
monthly expenses, 47, 50, 126
Mortgage Electronic Registration Systems, 61
Mortgage holder, 54
mortgage loan modification, 15
Mortgage originator, 54
Mortgage Rate Weekly Updates, 173
Mortgage servicer, 54
mortgage servicers, 10, 16, 31, 40, 80, 94, 96, 98, 99, 100, 102, 120
mortgage servicing companies, 9, 25, 43, 47, 79, 84, 153
net present value, 24, 113
Net Present Value Calculator, 173
non-judicial foreclosure, 154

©Robert Rodgers, PhD

Stop Foreclosure

NPV, 25, 93, 94, 96, 98, 99, 101, 102, 104, 107, 109, 110, 112, 113, 114, 116, 119, 120, 121
Partial Reinstatement, 160
penalties, 29, 44, 45, 58, 59, 122, 145
phone representative, 13, 36, 38, 39, 40, 46, 70, 83, 85, 97, 98, 166
Power of Sale, 156
principal, 87, 90, 92, 95, 100, 140, 144, 150
Reinstatement, 161
Rejection Letter, 125
Repayment Plan, 160
Resources, 173
retirement fund, 41

savings account, 42, 167, 168
second job, 41, 119
Second Mortgage, 147
self-employed, 31, 33, 37, 40
Servicing agreements, 56
Short Sale, 162
Short-Term Forbearance, 137
Signs of a Scam, 68
social security, 33, 41
Strict Foreclosure, 157
Tax returns, 31
Temporary Loan Modification, 140
unemployment, 16, 34, 136, 137, 138
Unemployment, 8, 54, 136, 137
unemployment benefits, 34

www.ingramcontent.com/pod-product-compliance
Lightning Source LLC
Chambersburg PA
CBHW071759200526
45167CB00017B/466